Gymnastics

HEATHER E. SCHWARTZ

LUCENT BOOKS
A part of Gale, Cengage Learning

Detroit • New York • San Francisco • New Haven, Conn • Waterville, Maine • London

LIBRARY OF CONGRESS CATALOGING-IN-PUBLICATION DATA

Schwartz, Heather E.
    Gymnastics / by Heather E. Schwartz.
        p. cm. — (The science behind sports)
    Includes bibliographical references and index.
    ISBN 978-1-4205-0277-0 (hardcover)
    1. Gymnastics. I. Title.
    GV461.S418 2011
    796.4—dc22

                                                              2010033544

Lucent Books
27500 Drake Rd
Farmington Hills MI 48331

ISBN-13: 978-1-4205-0277-0
ISBN-10: 1-4205-0277-8

Printed in the United States of America
2 3 4 5 6 7 14 13 12 11

TABLE OF CONTENTS

FOREWORD

On March 21, 1970, Slovenian ski jumper Vinko Bogataj took a terrible fall while competing at the Ski-flying World Championships in Oberstdorf, West Germany. Bogataj's pinwheeling crash was caught on tape by an ABC *Wide World of Sports* film crew and eventually became synonymous with "the agony of defeat" in competitive sporting. While many viewers were transfixed by the severity of Bogataj's accident, most were not aware of the biomechanical and environmental elements behind the skier's fall—heavy snow and wind conditions that made the ramp too fast and Bogataj's inability to maintain his center of gravity and slow himself down. Bogataj's accident illustrates that, no matter how mentally and physically prepared an athlete may be, scientific principles—such as momentum, gravity, friction, and aerodynamics—always have an impact on performance.

Lucent Books' Science Behind Sports series explores these and many more scientific principles behind some of the most popular team and individual sports, including baseball, hockey, gymnastics, wrestling, swimming, and skiing. Each volume in the series focuses on one sport or group of related sports. The volumes open with a brief look at the featured sport's origins, history and changes, then move on to cover the biomechanics and physiology of playing, related health and medical concerns, and the causes and treatment of sports-related injuries.

In addition to learning about the arc behind a curve ball, the impact of centripetal force on a figure skater, or how water buoyancy helps swimmers, Science Behind Sports readers will also learn how exercise, training, warming up, and diet and nutrition directly relate to peak performance and enjoyment of the sport. Volumes may also cover why certain sports are popular, how sports function in the business world, and which hot sporting issues—sports doping and cheating, for example—are in the news.

Basic physical science concepts, such as acceleration, kinetics, torque, and velocity, are explained in an engaging and accessible manner. The full-color text is augmented by fact boxes, sidebars, photos, and detailed diagrams, charts and graphs. In addition, a subject-specific glossary, bibliography and index provide further tools for researching the sports and concepts discussed throughout Science Behind Sports.

CHAPTER **1**

An Ancient Sport

Today the word *gymnastics* evokes images of limber athletes performing amazing physical feats. Gymnastics is a sport that incorporates muscle strength, agility, and balance. Gymnasts demonstrate their abilities in each of these areas by performing specific moves, also called skills or tricks. Some basic gymnastics moves include the handstand, the forward roll, and the cartwheel.

Gymnasts compete in four disciplines to showcase their abilities: artistic gymnastics, rhythmic gymnastics, trampoline and tumbling, and acrobatics. Artistic gymnastics are performed on an apparatus, such as the balance beam, rings, or uneven bars. Rhythmic gymnastics take place on the floor, with gymnasts tossing and twirling ribbons, balls, and hoops. Trampoline and tumbling skills require elevated runways and trampolines that launch gymnasts high in the air. Acrobatic gymnastics are performed on the floor, and gymnasts work in pairs or groups.

In gymnastics every movement counts during a routine, or series of skills. In competitions judges award points for precision, style, and grace. The final trick gymnasts strive for in every routine is an impressive dismount from an apparatus, trampoline, or even another gymnast. When gymnasts land with total control, they earn more points that count toward their total score. "[Dismounts] encapsulate part of the sport's appeal—the idea of pushing the human body past its limits, of watching the human form distilled to its essence, lean and muscled, powerful and graceful, beautifully proportioned," writes author Joan Ryan in her book, *Little Girls in Pretty Boxes*. "Yet gymnastics, particularly the soaring, twisting dismounts, also attracts us for less aesthetic reasons, the same reasons we thrill to the circus performer lunging for the swinging trapeze—the wonderful and terrible possibilities of each death-defying moment."[1]

Pushing Beyond the Limits

Modern gymnasts' moves are undeniably precise, thrilling, dangerous, and inspiring. Many gymnasts who have gone on to become champions started out in the sport because they wanted to perform those impossible-looking moves themselves. "It wasn't visions of glory and stardom that captivated me," Olympic gymnast Kerri Strug admits. "It was the competition, and the spectacular tricks."[2]

Gymnastics tricks seem to push the human body beyond its limits. In reality, however, the moves work within biomechanical principles. Biomechanics is the science of how the body moves. It also refers to the effects of natural forces, such as gravity, on the body.

While gymnasts may be born with some genetic advantages or natural talents, they also train their bodies to stretch muscles and ligaments and improve flexibility. Training allows gymnasts to perform difficult tricks, such as the straddle split, which requires sitting with their legs to the sides of their body 180 degrees apart.

When gymnasts launch into the air, they may appear to overcome scientific forces, but they are once again adhering to them. While performing a vault, for example, gymnasts do not disprove the existence of gravity. Instead, they demonstrate an idea developed by Sir Issac Newton, a mathematician and physicist of the late seventeenth and early eighteenth centuries.

Newton developed three laws of motion. His first law says an object in motion tends to stay in motion unless it is stopped by another force. His second law says the acceleration of an object is related the force acting upon it. Newton's third law says for every action, there is an equal and opposite reaction.

During a vault, gymnasts run and jump hard onto a springboard in front of the apparatus (also called a vault). The force downward on the springboard creates an equal force upward, an example of Newton's third law. This opposite reaction helps gymnasts to gain height in the air despite the force of gravity pulling them down.

A Sport Is Born

In its earliest incarnation, gymnastics was not about perfecting specific skills and impressing spectators and judges with increasingly complex moves. Instead gymnasts focused on overall physical—and mental—fitness. The term *gymnastics* originally referred to a set of fitness activities that took place in the gymnasiums of ancient Greece from 8000 B.C. to 30 B.C.

Physical fitness was prized in ancient Greek culture as beneficial to overall health. Back then men and women practiced gymnastics by doing activities like running, jumping, swimming, wrestling, boxing, and lifting weights. Since they also believed in the importance of developing a healthy mind, ancient Greek citizens studied in gymnasiums as well. Subjects included music, math, and art.

Practicing gymnastic exercises, such as wrestling and boxing, prepared Greek citizens for battle. Gymnastics practice also got competitors ready for the Olympic Games, which originated in Greece in celebration of the god Zeus. The first recorded Olympic Games were held in 776 B.C., and they continued every four years until about A.D. 393. Modern gymnastics routines were not a part of the original games. Gymnastics at that time referred to activities such as running, wrestling, and throwing, which were included as events in the games.

While women were free to practice gymnastics, only men were allowed in early Olympic competitions. Athletes had to compete in the nude. Some experts believe this was to keep the competitions safe, since there was no clothing to trip over. Others say the ancient Greeks simply accepted nudity and celebrated the male physique. Nudity may also have been required so that male athletes could show off their fitness and form.

When Rome conquered Greece in 2 B.C., the Romans took up gymnastics themselves. They used the sport mainly as military training. The Olympic Games faded from existence and were eventually abolished in A.D. 393 by the Roman emperor Theodosius I. As a Christian, he did not support the Olympic Games' pagan origins. Centuries passed before gymnastics evolved into the modern sport known today.

The Evolution of Gymnastics

Modern gymnastics can be traced back to late eighteenth-century Germany. In 1793 German teacher Johann Christoph Friedrich GutsMuths published the book *Gymnastics for the Young*, detailing a program to improve balance, flexibility, and strength. That program formed the foundation for today's gymnastics.

Physical education teachers all over the world read GutsMuths's book and put it into practice with their students. Over hundreds of years, generations of students developed and evolved the sport according to different ideals, values, and beliefs about what constituted gymnastics and the best reasons to practice the sport.

Friedrich Ludwig Jahn, a German educator, was one of GutsMuths's readers. In 1811 he opened a gymnasium near Berlin, Germany, where he focused his training on building

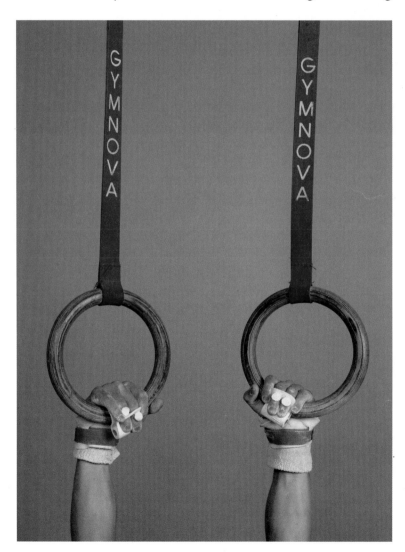

The father of modern gymnastics, Friedrich Ludwig Jahn, developed new equipment for the sport, such as the rings.

students' muscular strength. He developed special new equipment for his students to use, including a high bar, parallel bars, and rings. In addition, he developed an early balance beam. Today he is known as the father of modern gymnastics.

Franz Nachtegall, of Denmark, also read GutsMuths's book and went on to use gymnastics in the training of the Danish military. One of his students, Per Henrik Ling, of Sweden, developed the sport further by focusing on specific movements, body positions, and routines. Eventually some of his students took his teachings in a new direction. They went on to teach gymnastics that allowed athletes to express themselves with their moves, almost like dancers. This type of gymnastics could be considered an early form of rhythmic gymnastics.

The Modern Olympic Games

In 1881 representatives from gymnastics associations in Belgium, France, and Netherlands met to form what is now known as the Fédération Internationale de Gymnastique (International Gymnastics Federation). With an international governing organization, international gymnastic competitions could be held. Fifteen years later, gymnastics became an Olympic sport.

The first modern Olympic Games were held in 1896 in Athens, Greece. Competitors came from thirteen different countries to participate in the events, including rope climbing and vaulting. In the early years only male gymnasts were allowed to compete. Female gymnasts began competing in 1928.

Until 1984, artistic gymnastics was the only discipline represented at the Olympic Games. Modern artistic gymnastics incorporates several different events. Male gymnasts perform on the pommel horse, an apparatus made of a padded metal frame set on a stand, and the rings, which hang from cables attached to a tower. Female gymnasts perform on the balance beam, a 4-inch-wide (10cm) beam that stands 4 feet (1.2m) high.

All gymnasts perform on bars. Men compete on the parallel and horizontal bars, while women compete on the uneven bars. The gymnasts grip the bars and swing around them to

perform tricks. Floor and vault events are open to both male and female gymnasts. Floor routines include tumbling and acrobatic tricks. The vault is like a pommel horse but without handles and gymnasts launch over it using a springboard.

Throughout their routines, gymnasts use speed to gain momentum for height when flipping and to gain distance when leaping or jumping. Momentum is the measure of the motion of a body and its resistance to slowing down. It is calculated by multiplying mass by velocity. Gymnasts use muscle strength to maintain good form and control of each move. They demonstrate flexibility by bending and twisting to create unusual shapes with their bodies. They also use psychological strength to overcome natural anxieties and perform their impossible-looking skills.

The Competition Heats Up

In 1952 Russia made a huge impression at the Olympic Games in Helsinki, Finland. Both its men's and women's gymnastic teams won the gold medal. Plus many of the Russian gymnasts won gold, silver, and bronze medals for the individual events. Russia's gymnasts became known as the best in the world. Many of the best male gymnasts also came from Japan. Members of the team won silver and bronze medals at the 1952 Olympic Games.

By the 1960s Romania was gearing up to challenge the countries dominating gymnastics. A Romanian physical education teacher named Bela Karolyi started teaching gymnastics to girls in his country. At seven to eleven years old, his students were much younger than most competitive gymnasts, who were in their twenties and thirties.

Karolyi taught his students new kinds of gymnastic moves that emphasized physical strength. To build this strength, their training included lifting weights, running, and rope climbing. They also spent much more time practicing than other gymnasts. Karolyi's students won local and regional competitions and performed well in national competitions, gaining the government's attention. Soon Karolyi was asked to join a national effort to train Romania's first generation of gymnasts to compete at an international level. Karolyi had one goal in mind as a gymnastics coach: He wanted to beat the Russians.

For three years Karolyi trained young girls in gymnastics using his own methods to create superior athletes. In 1972 he took his team to an international competition. One of his students, Nadia Comaneci, won several events and helped them beat the Russians. "Everybody was shocked. It was considered an accident. Nobody could explain how we came away with a huge trophy," Karolyi says. "But our little team just bulldozed them down."[3]

Behind the Scenes: Nadia's Perfect Ten

When Nadia Comaneci earned her perfect scores at the 1976 Olympics, she felt she was simply doing her job and trying her best. While the scores came in, she performed on each apparatus, then warmed up to perform on the next. Her scores registered on the scoreboard as "1.0." No one had ever earned a perfect score in gymnastics, and the scoreboard could not display the numeral ten.

The world was amazed, but Comaneci took it all in stride. "It didn't have an impact on me—not one bit," she says. "I thought that maybe the judges were being too good to me. The team was happy about my scores, but none of us focused on them. We needed to pay attention to the rest of the competition."

Nadia Comaneci, *Letters to a Young Gymnast*, New York: Basic Books, 2004, p. 44.

In the 1976 Olympics, Nadia Comaneci was the first gymnast to earn a perfect score.

Later at the 1976 Olympic Games, Comaneci was fourteen years old when she became the first gymnast in Olympic history to score a perfect ten. Under the system of scoring at that time, Comaneci performed routines that were worth a maximum of ten points. If she had made mistakes, points would have been deducted. Instead she earned seven perfect ten scores during the competition. Two of the moves she performed were new and named for her: the Comaneci salto and the Comaneci dismount.

Signature Tricks

Modern elite gymnasts do not just perform difficult skills. They invent new ones. The Comaneci Salto is performed on the uneven bars. The gymnast does a giant swing on the high bar then releases it to flip in a front tuck in the air before recatching the bar.

"I always wanted to do the impossible, so when Bela [Karolyi] came up with the idea for the Comaneci Salto, I was eager to try to perfect the skill," Comaneci says. "A similar move was already being performed from the low bar to the high bar. Bela thought I could do it all on the high bar by catching the same bar I'd released. I spent countless hours, days, weeks, and months perfecting the never before attempted skill."[4]

Japanese gymnast Mitsuo Tsukahara, a star at the 1968, 1972, and 1976 Olympic Games, invented the Tsukahara vault. He jumped off the springboard and did a half twist before pushing off the horse backward. Russian gymnast Olga Korbut, who dominated the 1972 Olympics, invented the Korbut salto, a backward aerial somersault performed on the balance beam, and the Korbut flip, a backflip performed on the uneven bars.

In 1983 another Russian gymnast, Natalia Yurchenko, introduced a difficult new vault at the World Gymnastics Championships. To perform the move, Yurchenko ran toward the vault, then did a round off to land facing backward on a springboard. She launched off the springboard, and as she went over the vault, she touched it with her hands. Pushing off, she performed a twist in the air before landing.

The move required speed, momentum, and especially control, because it was riskier than other moves on the vault. Landing backward meant Yurchenko could not see the vault. She risked misplacing her hands and hitting her head at a high speed.

The rush to beat the competition was on. By the 1984 Olympic Games, "the Yurchenko" had become a standard move that all gymnasts incorporated into their routines. "Yurchenko had trained for years to perfect the vault, but young American girls had to learn it almost overnight to keep pace with the Soviets," writes Ryan.[5]

As gymnastics became more competitive, the sport developed and changed for future gymnasts. In addition to new skills, new gymnastics disciplines were introduced in competition. Rhythmic gymnastics, which are performed on the floor, became an Olympic event at the 1984 games. Only female gymnasts compete in rhythmic gymnastics, using

THE YURCHENKO VAULT AND ITS VARIATIONS

Performed for the first time in 1983 by Natalia Yurchenko, a Yurchenko vault is any vault maneuver that begins with a round-off cartwheel onto the springboard, and then a back handspring to the horse. Gymnasts then add their own variations by performing twists and saltos (somersaults). The vault illustrated below is known as a 2 ½ Twisting Yurchenko Vault, and is notorious for its complexity.

Back handspring onto vault

Run toward vault

Double back flip salto with 2 ½ twists

Round-off cartwheel onto springboard

Sticks two-footed landing

music as well as ribbons, balls, and hoops to accompany their moves. They use muscle strength to point their toes, keep their legs straight and tight, and control their form so each move is precisely executed. They demonstrate flexibility with splits that extend their legs 180 degrees or more. In order to earn points, their performance also needs unique choreography. Their jumps, pivots, leaps, balances, and flexibility are all evaluated for their final score.

Trampoline was introduced as an Olympic event in the 2000 games. In this event athletes bounce on a trampoline. With each bounce the gymnasts perform a new trick, maintaining balance and control until they halt their momentum and land with both feet on the trampoline bed.

Gymnasts performing on the trampoline are judged on their form in three positions. Throughout a performance they generally keep their arms straight whether in a tucked position, a piked position, or a straight position. In a tuck, knees are bent. In a piked position, gymnasts' legs must be straight and angled less than 135 degrees from the hip. In a straight position, gymnasts' legs must also be straight, angled more than 135 degrees from the hip.

Changing Rules

While the skills and disciplines of competitive gymnastics have evolved over time, the rules for competing have changed as well. When Karolyi began churning out young champions, female gymnasts in their twenties and thirties had no chance against them. The new top gymnasts, who had not yet reached puberty, were smaller and more flexible.

In 2008 Nellie Kim, an Olympic gymnast who later worked for the International Gymnastics Federation, told the *New York Times* that younger gymnasts benefit from being lighter than their competition. "It's easier to do tricks," she said. "And psychologically, I think they worry less."[6]

Age is not as much of an issue for male gymnasts. In their book *Kurt Thomas on Gymnastics* Olympic gymnast Kurt Thomas and author Kent Hannon comment on the issue of size in the sport. They write, "In gymnastics, small is beautiful. The Japanese have proved that axiom by fielding the shortest, lightest and best men's gymnastics teams since

ROUND OFF

33 years

Age of Oksana Chusovitina the oldest female gymnast competing at the 2008 Olympic Games. She competed for Germany and won a silver medal in vault.

1960. Their gold-medal-winning team at the 1976 Olympics averaged five feet three (160 cm) and 130 pounds (59 kg), the most diminutive lineup of any country."[7]

Some feared gymnastics was developing into a sport in which only children could compete on the elite level. Many talented gymnasts would be edged out if the age of competitors dropped lower and lower in order to produce smaller athletes. Rules were soon enacted that set minimum ages for gymnasts competing in the Olympics.

Before 1981, the minimum age for female gymnastics competitors in the Olympic Games was fourteen. The minimum age was sixteen for male gymnasts. In 1997, however, the mi nimum age was raised to sixteen for all gymnasts. During the 2008 Olympic Games in Beijing, China, controversy erupted over the age of one gymnast. The news media reported Chinese gymnast He Kexin's age as thirteen, which led to questions about the ages of other gymnasts on her

Chinese gymnast He Kexin (pictured) caused controversy in the 2008 Olympic Games when the media reported that she was 13 years old— three years younger than the minimum age set for gymnasts in 2000.

team. Some people thought the Chinese gymnasts were exceptionally small and looked too young to be sixteen year olds. On average, they were 4 feet, 9 inches tall (1.4m) and weighed 77 pounds (35kg).

After the Chinese women's team won a total of two gold medals and two bronze medals, the International Gymnastics Federation determined the gymnasts' documents proved they were old enough to compete. Still, the controversy raised questions about cheating and highlighted the fact that gymnastics had become a sport where youth and size could give gymnasts an edge, both physically and mentally. In a 2008 article for *Sports Illustrated* sportswriter Selena Roberts writes, "Age has a lot to do with what's level in gymnastic competitions. There is a mental advantage for youngsters who are clueless about pressure, unaware of what wobbles the burden to win can create."[8]

A New Scoring System

In response to disputes over judging at the 2004 Olympic Games, a new scoring system was adopted for the sport. Gymnasts now receive two scores, one on the difficulty of their routine and the other on their execution of the skills. The scores are combined, and a high score is usually in the range of sixteen to seventeen, or slightly higher.

The new scoring was introduced at the 2008 Olympics, but not everyone in the gymnastics community was happy about the change. Under the new system, gymnasts no longer had the potential to earn a perfect ten. "It was something that I grew up with and when I think of 10.0, it's perfection," Olympic gymnast Morgan Hamm told Bloomberg news. "It was disappointing when they changed the system. It would be nice if it was still here but the sport keeps evolving."[9]

In some sports mathematical formulas based on ideas developed by Sir Issac Newton can predict performance and work as a basis for scoring. According to Jordan Ellenberg, a writer for the online magazine Slate,

> there are some Olympic sports in which an upper limit might be more appropriate than in gymnastics—in sprinting, for instance, where today's fastest runners

Scoring Modern Gymnastics

Many critics worry that the new scoring system encourages gymnasts to go too far in delivering dangerous tricks to impress judges. Gymnast Nastia Liukin, for example, learned a bars routine specifically designed by her father and coach to earn a high score at the U.S. Gymnastics Championships. At the time, she was also preparing for the 2008 Olympic Games.

"I was like: 'Wow, you want me to do all of that? Is that possible?'" she said in an interview with the *New York Times*. "But then I realized that I need to do all that with this new scoring, if I even want to think about a gold medal. I said: 'OK, cool. I'll learn it.'"

Quoted in Juliet Macur, "A 10 Isn't Necessarily Perfect in New Scoring System for Gymnastics," *New York Times*, August 6, 2008, www.nytimes.com/2008/08/06/sports/olympics/06scoring.html?pagewanted=all

may actually be very close to the absolute physical limits of human ability.... Gymnastics, by contrast, isn't constrained by simple applications of Newtonian mechanics. Gymnasts can perform moves that no one's carried out before—that no one ever *thought* of carrying out before.[10]

By indicating exactly how judges should award and deduct points, the new scoring system became less subjective than the old.

The sport of gymnastics has changed and developed over centuries. There is no doubt gymnastics will continue to evolve. New skills, new disciplines, and new methods to judge push gymnasts beyond what their predecessors could do. Today gymnasts harness scientific forces and build specific muscle strength and flexibility to achieve performances once thought impossible.

CHAPTER 2

Training and Conditioning

Some say gymnastics demands the fittest of athletes. Performing in this sport requires that gymnasts develop a unique combination of flexibility, muscle strength, and endurance. This high level of fitness allows the athletes to use their bodies to overcome the biomechanical challenges encountered while performing tricks.

One of these challenges is making rotations off of an apparatus like the balance beam or the bars. For example, gymnasts use their bodies to create angular momentum during a spin or rotation. Angular momentum is a force of motion that keeps an object in rotation.

Gymnasts create angular momentum while spinning by tucking chin to chest, pulling their arms in, and pulling their knees up to their chest. Through these actions, they are decreasing their inertia. Inertia is a measurement that describes a body's resistance to change. If a body is in motion, it will remain in motion in a straight line, and if it is at rest, it will remain at rest, unless acted upon by an outside force. By altering the way their body weight is distributed, gymnasts can spin faster because a compact object is less resistant to an increase in speed. "Things with their weight spread out tend to resist changes more," says Dustyn Roberts, a sports biomechanics researcher at the Center for Podiatric

Care and Sports Medicine in New York City. "This is why you put your arms out when trying to balance on a balance beam. It spreads out your weight and makes you less likely to tip over."[11]

Intense Training

To be able to perform such tricks, however, gymnasts need to train. Training focuses on practicing skills over and over. Repetition helps gymnasts move ahead in the sport in part because practice trains the brain. With every repetition of a move, the brain learns to use more parts of muscles and to use muscles in new ways so they are more efficient. Practice also improves flexibility and strengthens the muscles required for specific gymnastic skills.

Gymnastics workouts can be intense, whether gymnasts are just starting out, veterans of the sport, or trying to make a comeback. Many gymnasts start young and train for several hours each week. Olympic gymnast Mary Lou Retton remembers how her training with famed gymnastics coach Bela Karolyi began. In her 1986 book, *Mary Lou: Creating an Olympic Champion* that she coauthored with Karolyi, she writes,

> My first workout at Karolyi's was on a Sunday afternoon, and that's always the toughest of the week. I started on bars, and Bela had me doing new skills right away, things I'd never even tried that the other girls had been working

Dressing for Success

Whether warming up, working out, or competing, gymnasts wear specific outfits to enhance their performance. Female gymnasts traditionally wear a long-sleeved leotard. They are also allowed to wear a sleeveless leotard in competition. Male gymnasts traditionally wear a sleeveless leotard with shorts or pants. Gymnastics leotards are made of stretchy material, so they will not hinder gymnasts' movements. The outfits are formfitting, so coaches and judges can see how gymnasts move and create body shapes.

Gymnastics outfits are designed to assist gymnasts, too. Heavier clothing could weigh them down when they attempt to launch into the air. Looser clothing could disrupt the air flow as they perform tricks, creating drag, or air resistance, which would slow them down as they try to run and leap through the air. Tight clothing helps gymnasts create an aerodynamic shape with their body, so they can slip through the air more easily. Air flows with less resistance over an object that is sleek and smooth.

on. Well, I was trying my hardest to impress everyone, and I was just killing myself, falling and bruising things but also making improvement. I wasn't going to cry and show Bela I was a baby, but it was so hard.[12]

Developing Flexibility

Gymnastics skills require athletes to stretch beyond normal range of motion. For example, most people who are not gymnasts cannot perform a straddle split, which requires sitting with the legs to the sides of the body 180 degrees apart. In order to work up to such a skill, every gymnast's workout schedule includes flexibility training. Stretches help

Since many gymnastics skills require athletes to stretch beyond normal range of motion, a gymnast's workout schedule includes flexibility training.

increase flexibility throughout the body, including hip and arm flexors and even fingers and toes. Stretching conditions not only the muscles, but also the tendons and ligaments that support joints, so they are prepared for gymnastics moves and not prone to injury.

In a static stretch to improve the straddle split, gymnasts sit in the split position with their legs as far out as they will go. In a dynamic stretch, gymnasts do the same, then contract their muscles and pull their legs back even further. They relax then repeat the contraction and pull back over and over to increase the stretch. The increase in flexibility comes from muscle tissue adapting to the stretch. Over time the muscle remodels itself into longer tissue, which allows for greater flexibility.

Gaining Muscle Strength

Gymnasts also need muscle strength to perform their moves. Many gymnastics tricks require quick bursts of intense energy to launch, twist, and flip in the air. For these types of skills, gymnasts need to develop fast-twitch muscle fibers. When they sprint toward the vault, for example, fast-twitch muscle fibers respond to nerve impulses from the brain by contracting quickly and forcefully. The fast muscle movement creates speed and the force of the contraction creates power.

Gymnasts condition fast-twitch muscle fibers through plyometric drills, such as jumps, which stretch and contract the muscles with added force. Plyometric drills are meant to overload muscle. This stimulates the brain to recruit more fast-twitch muscle fibers to work. With more fast-twitch muscle in use, a gymnast will gain speed and power and perform more efficiently.

Gymnasts also focus on strengthening their core muscles, which are needed for every move from pulling up on the bars to flipping on the balance beam. The core muscles include the abdominals and other muscles that stabilize the torso from the shoulders to the pelvis and along the spine. When gymnasts perform a handstand, for example, they tighten their core muscles to balance and hold their body in a straight line without tipping forward, backward, or to the

side. Gymnasts strengthen these muscles through exercises like sit-ups, crunches, and V sits.

In V sits, gymnasts sit with their back and legs straight. They use their abdominal muscles to lift their legs to a forty-five-degree angle. Then they reach forward to their shins for a deeper contraction. With their body in a V shape, gymnasts can work their rectus abdominus, obliques, and hip flexors. The muscle contractions stimulate more muscle tissue to grow. When muscles are challenged to the point of fatigue, they are slightly injured in the process. New cells repair them by increasing the thickness of the fibers, which makes them stronger.

Building Endurance

In addition to flexibility and muscle strength, gymnasts also need endurance, or staying power, to continue exerting themselves. Without endurance, gymnasts lose energy, which means they lose the physical capacity to do work. In that case, they cannot perform well, even during a floor routine that lasts only sixty to ninety seconds. "It sounds like a short time, but it's a long time to perform skills,"[13] says Kim Rhatigan-Drexler, a high school gymnastics coach and a gymnastics coordinator and member of the New York State Public High School Gymnastics Committee.

Athletes use slow-twitch muscle fibers to perform physical activity for long periods of time. Compared to fast-twitch muscle fibers, slow-twitch muscle fibers contract more slowly. Slow-twitch muscle fibers are used during cardiovascular exercises, such as running, jumping jacks, and a variety of other aerobic exercises. Through prolonged cardiovascular exercise, the muscles adapt to the work and become better able to tolerate it.

Fueling Muscles

Gymnasts know they are going to work hard when they go into the gym for a training session. It is extremely important for them to avoid dehydration. Muscle tissue needs water to function, since it is made of about 75 percent water. Dehydration can adversely affect mental concentration, how the body regulates temperature, and muscular performance. Small amounts of fluid throughout a workout session help gymnasts replenish body fluids lost through sweating.

Gymnasts also know they have to provide the fuel that will get their bodies

ROUND OFF

1,200

The daily amount of calories in Olympic gymnast Nastia Liukin's diet while she was training for the 2008 Olympic Games.

through the intense workout. Fuel for a gymnast's body means eating foods that contain proteins and carbohydrates. Without the proper nutrients, gymnasts cannot build the muscles they need to perform. Their bodies will be weak and lack energy, endurance, and power.

In order to provide fast-twitch muscle fibers with the glycogen they use for energy, gymnasts need to eat carbohydrates. Carbohydrates break down during digestion and create sugars, including glycogen, in the body. There are two types of carbohydrates: simple and complex. Simple carbohydrates break down very quickly and are found in foods like fruit and yogurt. They provide a burst of energy that does not last long. Gymnasts benefit more by loading up on complex carbohydrates, which are found in whole wheat pasta and vegetables. Complex carbohydrates break down more slowly, so the energy they provide lasts longer.

Gymnasts also get energy from lean protein, which is found in fish and chicken. During digestion, protein is broken down into amino acids. Amino acids are used to build and replenish the muscle tissue gymnasts need to perform tricks. Excess amino acids are metabolized into glycogen, which can

Gymnastics Levels

As gymnasts learn new skills and progress in the sport, they are ranked from one to ten. Level one is for beginners. Elite gymnasts are at level ten. These gymnasts are qualified to try out for teams that will go to international competitions, such as the Olympic Games.

USA Gymnastics, a governing organization that sets rules and standards for gymnastics in the United States, set the standards that determine how a gymnast should be ranked. Coaches and competition scores determine when a gymnast can advance to the next level. Gymnasts do have some control over their progress, however. With hard work and determination, they can learn new skills quickly. Many gymnasts speed up the process by competing at more than one level during a single year.

be used for energy. Protein is also converted into adenosine triphosphate (ATP), a source of energy for muscles.

A diet high in protein and low in carbohydrates is common for gymnasts at the elite level. Olympic gymnast Nadia Comaneci learned to eat that way when she began training with Bela Karolyi in the 1970s. "Our meals were all very regimented—mostly grilled meat, fish, and salads and fruit. We didn't eat any pastas or bread because the team doctor didn't believe they were important components of a well-balanced meal," she says. "The doctor designed a menu based on what each week demanded nutritionally, such as protein, vegetables, fruit, and milk. Meals were not about enjoyment but about nutrients."[14]

Training Starts Early for Elites

Like many elite gymnasts, Comaneci was very young when she began her gymnastics career. She was only six years old when Karolyi spotted her potential and recruited her as a student at his gym in 1967. Decades later, Olympic gymnasts were still beginning training at a young age. Olympic gymnasts and twins Paul Hamm and Morgan Hamm, for example, started gymnastics at age seven.

Even today elite gymnasts start training before they reach puberty. Many coaches believe that it is a good time to maximize their potential, because they have less body mass than they will have when they grow up. Body mass refers to how much space gymnasts' bodies occupy as well as how much they weigh. It takes less energy for lighter, more streamlined gymnasts to launch into the air to perform tricks.

Because they have less surface area, smaller gymnasts also encounter less resistance as they move through the air. Air resists objects moving through it, pushing against them, and creating drag. Drag causes objects to decelerate, or slow down.

ROUND OFF
1963

The year USA Gymnastics was established to oversee gymnastics in the United States. The organization's responsibilities include setting rules and policies, educating coaches, and selecting and training gymnasts for the Olympic Games and World Championships.

Elite gymnasts start training at an early age—often before they reach puberty.

When they land, smaller gymnasts create less force upon impact, allowing them to maintain their balance better. When gymnasts are not balanced, their weight is not distributed evenly, and they could easily step out of position or fall.

Psychologically young gymnasts also tend to be more dedicated to the sport. They may be more willing than adults to trust authority figures, such as coaches. Some people in the gymnastics community believe younger gymnasts have less experience with failure and may not fully understand the physical risks they are taking.

Training Too Hard?

Many top gymnasts today train between twenty-five and forty hours each week. They practice skills and routines over and over so the moves become natural and efficient and use less energy to perform. They also work with sports psychologists to prepare for the pressure of competing.

Some gymnasts become so dedicated to the sport that they take extreme measures to stay competitive. They might train more than their bodies can handle, risking injury to muscles, joints, and bones. While there are coaches who encourage this kind of rigorous training, most put their athletes' health first. Leading up to the 2008 Olympics, American gymnast Shawn Johnson's coach had her train ten to fifteen fewer hours each week than elites have traditionally trained. That kept the gymnast from burning out physically or emotionally. She became a role model when she won four medals at the Olympics.

Elite gymnasts, especially female gymnasts, have also developed a reputation of trying to stay as light and lean as children so they will be more competitive. To keep themselves from gaining weight—or even entering puberty— some have starved themselves. Other gymnasts have developed the habit of purging or abusing laxatives to keep their bodies from fully digesting the food that they eat. This type of dangerous behavior can lead to serious health complications and even death.

While male gymnasts are also under pressure, they are not known for developing these types of habits on such a mass scale. In his book *Kurt Thomas on Gymnastics* which he coauthored with Kent Hannon, Thomas reflects on gender differences in training and performing in gymnastics as a twenty-two-year-old elite gymnast in the 1970s. He writes,

> It's odd, but girls' success in gymnastics often depends on physical and emotional immaturity. As they grow up and develop women's bodies, they usually lose some

of that precious flexibility and acquire other interests. At my age [22], most women gymnasts are washed up. Boys are just the opposite. They can't do great things until they begin to get strong and coordinated and until their confidence starts to flow. A man can remain at top form until he's thirty.[15]

Banishing the Myth

The curves of the human body can affect a gymnast's performance. Objects that are not streamlined create air resistance and drag, which slows their motion through space. A small body type, however, does not always provide a competitive edge for gymnasts. The lack of larger muscles can actually be a disadvantage in performing skills that require speed and power. For example, gymnasts use their muscles to gain speed when running toward the vault. Speed creates energy that helps them launch into the air and gain distance and height. Height is needed to perform flips and twists properly before landing, and gymnasts are judged on the distance and height they achieve. A more impressive performance will earn them points in competition regardless of their size.

Small size is not necessarily an advantage on the balance beam either, at least when it comes to foot size. Larger

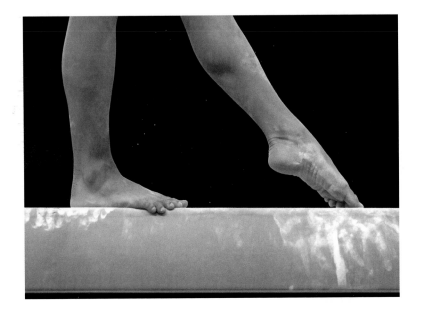

Small is not always an advantage in gymnastics. Larger feet can provide more stability for an athlete on the balance beam.

feet actually provide more stability than small feet. "From a biomechanical perspective, larger feet that turn out offer a gymnast a more solid base of support to perform the activities that are necessary on a balance beam," explains Matthew Goodemote, a physical therapist. "When our feet angle out this increases the width of our base of support. Larger feet also increase the surface and contact area, which in turn improves our base of support. These two factors are important components for a good base of support and make sticking a landing much easier."[16]

Body type and size are not the sole determining factors for success in gymnastics, however. And gymnasts never need to abuse their bodies to win. Working out and conditioning can help gymnasts excel no matter what their size. As a short gymnast with a stocky build, Retton is a perfect example. She will always be known as the first American woman to win a gold medal in gymnastics.

CHAPTER 3

Somersaults, Headstands, and Other Beginner Moves

E ven the most talented gymnasts start out by learning basic gymnastic movements. Beginners in the sport learn to create basic body shapes, such as the straddle split, the bridge, and the headstand. They learn simple acrobatic movements, like somersaults and cartwheels. They learn to place one foot in front of the other and walk in a straight line with perfect balance. At first these skills are practiced and performed on the floor.

Basic skills are a foundation gymnasts can learn from, build on, and use over and over—even at the elite level. While these beginner moves may look simple, they are not easy to master. Perfecting the basics requires balance, flexibility, coordination, and strength, the same as more advanced skills. In fact, the basics are the building blocks for learning more difficult skills in gymnastics.

Gymnastics Apparatus

Entering a gymnastics gym for the first time, new gymnasts get their first look at all the apparatus they will learn to use. Throughout the gym mats are used to protect gymnasts from the hard floor. The mats are located under and around apparatus and are placed in open areas for floor routines. Without mats, headstands, somersaults, and other moves would certainly be uncomfortable, and a fall off an apparatus could cause injury or even be fatal.

Mats used for gymnastics come in many different sizes, but they do have to meet certain criteria to serve their purpose. They have to be heavy enough that they will not slide away when gymnasts land on them. They also need to be thick enough to provide a cushion when gymnasts land from skills that send them airborne. Landing puts major stress on muscles, joints, and bones. Even tumbling exercises are tough on the body when a gymnast practices them repeatedly to get them right. A softer surface created by a mat helps lessen the impact. Tumbling mats are typically made

Springboards can help a gymnast reach the bars, launch over the vaulting table, or mount the balance beam.

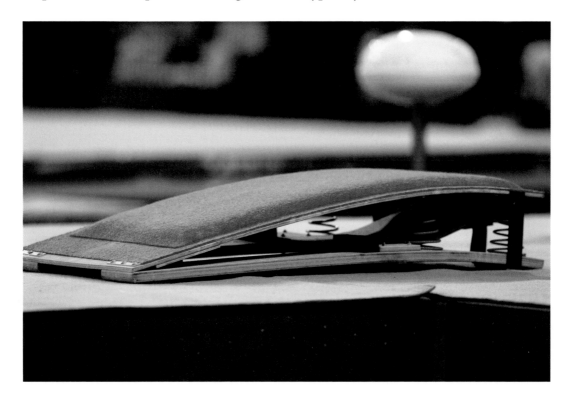

of foam covered in vinyl. They are generally between 1 and 2.5 inches (2.5cm and 6.4cm) thick. Landing mats for use with airborne tricks are 4.7 to 7.9 inches (12cm to 20cm) thick.

A springboard is another piece of equipment that help gymnasts perform. It can be used to launch over the vault, mount the balance beam, or reach the bars. Springboards are made of two boards with several springs between them. When gymnasts jump down on a springboard, they create mechanical energy that is stored in the springs. When gymnasts jump up off the springboard, the stored energy exerts force to propel them with more power and height than they could create on their own.

Warming Up

Before gymnasts begin any gymnastic moves, however, they need to prepare their bodies by warming up. Warm-up exercises literally warm up the entire nervous system, which includes the brain, spinal cord, and nerves throughout the body. The exercises also increase blood flow to muscles, warming them up and relaxing tissues so they will stretch more easily.

Gymnasts usually do aerobic exercises to begin a warm-up, such as jogging or using a stationary bike. These aerobic activities increase body temperature, heart rate, and circulation. Increased heart rate and circulation causes blood to flow faster, warming muscles and bringing oxygen and nutrients to muscles so the gymnast will have the energy to perform.

After the aerobic portion of a warm-up, gymnasts perform slow stretches to warm up specific areas of the body. They pay special attention to their back and hips, as well as their abdominal, leg, and arm muscles. Stretches improve range of motion and condition the tissues surrounding the joint. Stretches also circulate synovial fluid, a slippery lubricant that helps joints move more easily.

If gymnasts have a limited amount of time for a practice, most coaches would rather see them take less time to practice skills and routines and more time to stretch beforehand. "It is so important to stretch. If you don't warm up, it's a recipe for disaster," says Kim Rhatigan-Drexler, a high school gymnastics coach and a gymnastics coordinator and member of the New York State Public High School Gymnastics Committee. "You risk a bad injury."[17] Gymnasts who do not warm up could easily strain or pull a muscle. Groin injuries are particularly common when gymnasts fail to warm up. They also take a long time to heal.

By the end of a warm-up session, gymnasts have changed how their nervous system performs. Increased heart rate, breathing rate, and circulation raise body temperature and result in more blood and oxygen reaching the brain, spinal cord, and nerves to produce quicker reactions. The entire nervous system works faster to transmit impulses from the brain and spinal reflex center to muscles. The gymnast will be able to move and react faster while performing skills. Vaulting, for example, requires speed to create the force needed to launch the body into the air. Reaction time can also be critical when a gymnast has to make a split second adjustment of positioning in midair, while performing on the balance beam.

Calming Nerves

While warming up helps gymnasts prepare their muscles to perform, beginners may still move awkwardly at first. They may feel intimidated and nervous as well as excited. After all, even foundation skills put new gymnasts into unfamiliar circumstances. For example, they will try out potentially uncomfortable positions when they create body shapes on the floor. They will experience height when they try out the balance beam, rings, and bars.

Nervous gymnasts tense their muscles, so their movements are stiff instead of agile. Stiff, jerky movements also make a gymnast more likely to fall. Even worse, gymnasts who are new to the sport instinctively try to break falls by sticking out their arms. The common result is injury to the arms, hands, or wrists when the force of impact bends them into positions they would not normally go. Ligaments may tear and bones could even break.

In order to combat nerves, new gymnasts need to gain confidence. Feeling confident helps gymnasts concentrate, relax muscles throughout their body, and conserve energy. When muscles are relaxed, they contract more effectively

than tight, stiff muscles to help the gymnast create smooth, controlled movements. In the end, relaxed gymnasts are agile and able to perform better and therefore not as likely to fall.

Knowing how to fall safely, however, can also help a new gymnast gain confidence. Beginner gymnasts are taught to put their arms up instead of out when they fall. With practice, they automatically bend at the hips, knees, and ankles during a fall and roll to the floor to protect their limbs. The mats spread throughout the gym can make beginners feel more secure, too.

Stiff, jerky movements caused by nerves make a gymnast more likely to fall.

Moving Through Space

When new gymnasts begin to practice new moves, they are not always sure what they are doing or where they are going. This can be another source of anxiety for beginners, and they use their sense of vision to check the positioning of their arms, hands, legs, and other body parts. A large wall mirror

MOVING THROUGH SPACE

When gymnasts perform their routines, they are operating within three planes of motion (sagittal, frontal, and transverse) and around three axes of movement (transverse, medial, and longitudinal). Planes divide the body into left and right, front and back, and top and bottom, while axes are used to determine the rotational movement of the body. For instance, when performing a backflip a gymnast would be moving within the sagittal plane, going backwards, and bending or rotating the body at the frontal axis.

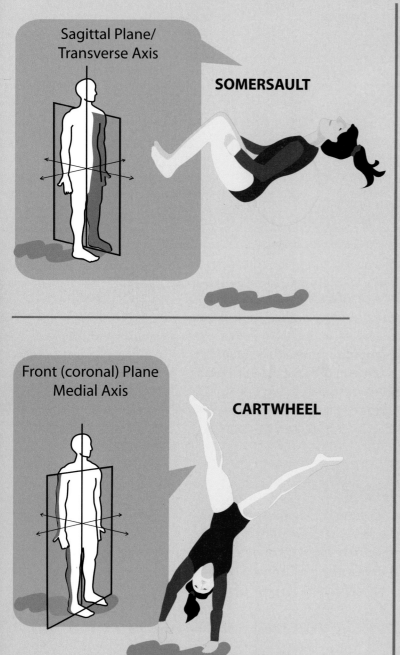

Sagittal Plane/
Transverse Axis

SOMERSAULT

Front (coronal) Plane
Medial Axis

CARTWHEEL

Transverse Plane/
Longitudinal
(vertical) Axis

TWIST

can help them as they develop their proprioception, or sense of orientation in space.

As they practice movements and skills, beginners improve their ability to understand feedback from proprioceptors in their muscles, joints, ligaments, tendons, and inner ears. Proprioceptors are nerve fibers that detect motion and positions of the body and deliver that information to the central nervous system. With experience, gymnasts gain a sense of what their body is doing as they move, without depending on sight alone.

Olympic gymnast Mary Lou Retton remembers learning to perform on the bars before she was accustomed to using her proprioception. In her book *Mary Lou: Creating an Olympic Champion*, she writes, "The first few times everything's so new you don't have any sense of where you are. You're eight feet off the ground on the high bar, and if you're in the middle of a routine and feel yourself falling, you see the low bar coming and you're worrying whether you're going to crack your head."[18]

New gymnasts also learn to sense their center of gravity and understand how it relates to balance. The center of gravity is the point in a gymnast's body where weight is evenly distributed. In order to maintain balance, a gymnast's body weight must be positioned evenly over the supporting body part or parts, such as feet, knees, or hands. As they move, gymnasts continually shift their weight to stay balanced while performing skills.

Beginners start learning balance by working on tumbling exercises, acrobatic moves performed on the floor. When they crouch to perform rolls, for example, their center of gravity is lower on their body than it is when they are standing. A low center of gravity is more stable, so they are less likely to fall over.

Rotating on the Axes

In addition to balance, tumbling also helps beginners learn the three axes of movement. All motion, including gymnastics skills, takes place on the transverse axis, the longitudinal axis, or the medial axis. Each axis is an imaginary line

Advancing to Compete

Beginners often start out by taking lessons at a gym or gymnastics club. Many gyms offer classes for students as young as eighteen months old. As gymnasts learn new skills in each discipline they move through levels established by USA Gymnastics, a governing body that oversees gymnastics rules and competitions. The progression on floor builds from learning rolling movements first to mastering cartwheels, handstands and salto skills. On bars, gymnasts learn static movements first, then progress to learning how to swing.

By the time they are four years old, many gymnasts can perform skills at USA Gymnastics' levels one and two. When gymnasts reach levels four and five, they often start competing against other gymnasts locally, regionally, and statewide. At competitions, also called meets, gymnasts show off their skills and battle for points by performing for judges. When gymnasts reach level 10, they are ready to try to qualify for elite competitions, like the Olympic Games.

By the time many gymnasts are four years old, they can perform at Levels 1 and 2 according to the USA Gymnastics standards.

running through a gymnast's center of gravity. Gymnasts perform by moving over and around these lines.

The transverse axis runs horizontally across the waist. Somersaults and backflips, among the first new skills a gymnast learns, are performed on the transverse axis. In a front somersault, a gymnast squats on the floor, tucks chin to chest, and rolls forward, returning to the starting position. Gymnasts use proprioception to stay in a straight line, so that eventually they can perform this skill at a more advanced level, such as on a balance beam.

A backflip is just what it sounds like—a flip backward through the air. Beginners are taught to swing their arms back to gain momentum and jump hard to get in the air. A spotter can help beginners jump high enough, rotate all the way around, and land on their feet.

Headstands and handstands are beginner skills performed on the longitudinal axis. The longitudinal axis runs vertically from head to toe. In a headstand gymnasts balance upside down, straighten their legs, and tighten abdominal and back muscles to keep in a straight line. Most beginners learn this skill by balancing up against a wall first. The wall acts as a support, so they can develop proper form and strengthen the muscles that will eventually help them balance in a freestanding position.

The handstand is similar to a headstand, except the gymnast's arms are straight with locked elbows, so all body weight rests on the hands, wrists, and arms. With enough practice, gymnasts eventually learn to walk on their hands.

A cartwheel is a rotation on the medial axis. The medial axis runs from back to front through the torso. The gymnast keeps arms and legs locked straight so the body forms an X shape. Then the gymnast rotates headfirst either to the left or the right. Body weight is supported on each hand while the gymnast is upside down and rotates back to the starting position.

Each basic skill a new gymnast learns can eventually be incorporated into a gymnastics routine. Routines are performed for an audience or for judges. They link several skills together, and more skills mean a more impressive performance. Gymnasts with a passion for the sport work hard to perfect the fundamentals that will help them win competitions and develop into elite athletes.

Practice Makes Perfect

Olympic gymnast Nadia Comaneci remembers making that journey herself, when she trained with coach Bela Karolyi as a child. In her 2004 book, *Letters to a Young Gymnast*, she writes,

> It took months to learn the simplest skills; a cartwheel on the beam began as one on a mat, then on a line painted on the floor, then on a low beam surrounded

by cushions, and finally moved to the high beam. Every day, I'd return to the gym and start all over again until I mastered each skill. I didn't mind because each step, repetition, loss, or gain made me better.... I was not born a champion and I did not dream in those early days of becoming one.... I dreamed of learning new skills.... [The basics] are the most important building blocks of a gymnastics career.[19]

Many who watched Comaneci perform perfectly in the 1976 Olympics might believe she was born with her abilities. But even for elite gymnasts, practice is the key to perfecting skills and tricks. As a child, Comaneci practiced gymnastics four to

For athletes, especially elite gymnasts, practice is the key to perfecting skills.

Nadia Comaneci's Early Years

Coach Bela Karolyi chose Nadia Comaneci for his gymnastics school after he saw her perform a cartwheel on a playground. At first she attended the school six days a week, spending four hours in regular classes, such as math and chemistry, and about four in the gym. Later she lived at the school in a dormitory with other gymnasts. They led a disciplined life, followed a strict diet, and went to bed every night by 10 P.M.

The structure helped the gymnasts improve their gymnastics skills, but Comaneci grew restless as she got older. She left the school and found a more lenient coach. Comaneci now had time to go to movies and discos. She tried treats she had never been allowed to eat before, like ice cream. The novelty of her new life was exciting, but after a few months she was out of shape, overweight, and unhappy. By 1978, she was back to training with Karolyi, running, working with weights, and following a balanced diet. Her outstanding performance at the European Championships in 1979 proved she had made a comeback.

six hours a day. In the beginning she was not a top performer, but she worked hard to improve. When her team worked out, she got double the practice in the same amount of time by doing six moves in the time it took other gymnasts to do three.

Other athletes put the same kind of time and dedication into the sport. When Olympic gymnast Blaine Wilson wanted to make it on the 2008 U.S. Olympic team, he spent about a year practicing five hours a day, five days a week, training with weights three of those days. Olympic gymnast Kerri Strug practiced eight hours a day throughout her gymnastics career, which lasted more than fourteen years. Shawn Johnson was at the gym four hours a day Monday through Friday and five to six hours on Saturday leading up to her gold medal win at the Olympics in 2008.

Muscle Memory

When gymnasts first learn new skills, they must think consciously about the muscles and movements required to perform them. They are aware of each step it takes to create a backflip or a cartwheel. With practice, however, muscle memory takes over. "When you repeat a motion over and over and over, your brain learns to perform that movement without really thinking about it. Your memory is in your brain, but your muscles also get used to performing the motion. Muscle memory refers to that phenomenon,"[20] explains Dustyn Roberts, a sports biomechanics researcher at the Center for Podiatric Care and Sports Medicine in New York City.

Some experts believe that, over time, information about muscle movement becomes an unconscious activity controlled by the part of the brain called the cerebellum. At that point, it could be said that muscle memory begins to work. Walking is an example of a physical activity controlled by the cerebellum. As babies learn to walk, they struggle to make their muscles move where they want to go. Adults, however, do not have to focus their energy and concentrate in order to walk down the street. They have been walking for so long that they just do it without consciously considering each muscle they need to move.

CHAPTER 4

Flying High

O nce gymnasts have mastered basic skills, they are literally ready to soar to greater heights. Many of the more difficult gymnastics moves send gymnasts into the air, spinning and flipping off apparatus like the bars, vault, and balance beam. In order to perform these tricks, experienced gymnasts need to use science to their advantage. They have to maximize speed, harness momentum, fight drag and friction, and challenge the force of gravity pulling them down to Earth.

Gaining Momentum

In a sense elite gymnasts are like trained fighters. They are taught to fight against forces that mean to keep them grounded. For example, gymnasts can defy gravity even from a standing position on the floor by creating enough of their own force to punch up into the air.

To perform a backflip, they start by putting their powerful leg muscles to work. They bend their knees, hips, and ankles and push off with their legs to jump into the air. This demonstrates principles of motion developed by mathematician and physicist Sir Issac Newton.

When gymnasts push down on the floor, an opposite force helps them launch up into the air, demonstrating Newton's third law of motion: For every action, there is an opposite and equal reaction. When gymnasts use their

THE PUNCH

To perform vault routines, gymnasts approach the spring board at a full run and leap onto the front section, over the springs. The forward momentum of the gymnast's body, running at maximum speed, is transferred into the board as downward force. The board pushes back on the body with an equal and opposite force, which is amplified by the compression and then recoil of the springs.

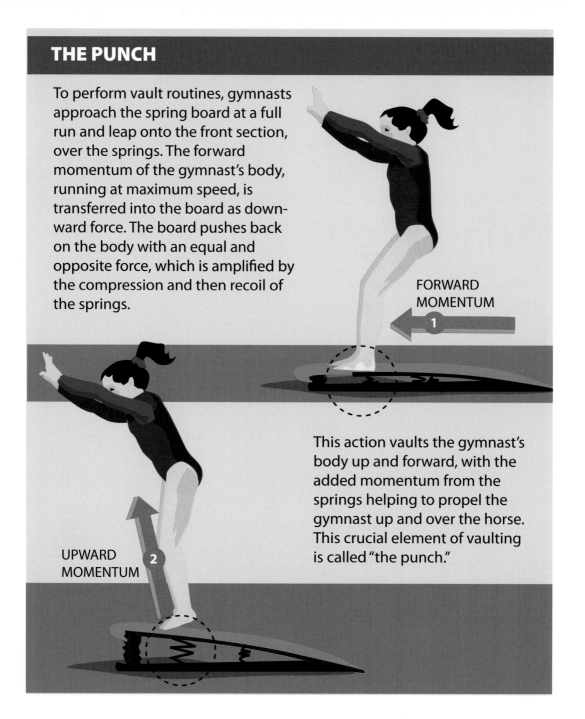

FORWARD MOMENTUM
1

UPWARD MOMENTUM
2

This action vaults the gymnast's body up and forward, with the added momentum from the springs helping to propel the gymnast up and over the horse. This crucial element of vaulting is called "the punch."

muscles to create force that accelerates motion, they demonstrate Newton's second law of motion: The acceleration of an object is related the force acting upon it. They also swing their arms back over their head to create backward momentum.

Gymnasts can also create forward momentum as well, such as when they run toward the vault to perform a trick. Forward momentum gives them the power to punch through the air when they land on the springboard and push off the vault. When a gymnast touches a surface, such as the vault, Newton's third law of motion is at work. When gymnasts push down on the vault with their hands, the vault does not collapse through the floor. Instead, it pushes up with equal force. That force helps to launch gymnasts into the air. "It can be frightening running full speed, knowing that if you mess up you're going to crash into the horse [vault]. So I can see where people get intimidated by it," Olympic gymnast Mary Lou Retton says. "But you still have to go full out because speed is the key. You're going horizontal and suddenly you have to punch it and go vertical, so you need all the momentum you can get."[21]

Fighting Friction and Other Forces

Kinetic energy, or the energy of motion, is not easy to stop. Still, while gymnasts try to gain speed and forward or backward momentum, other forces work to slow them down. When they run toward the vault, gymnasts fight against friction, which opposes forward motion and is created when their feet touch the floor. They also need to fight drag, a form of friction created when air particles come in contact with the gymnast's body. More force pushing objects together means more friction will result, such as during a vault when gymnasts touch the floor with their feet and push off the vault with their hands. The force at these points of contact creates friction and resistance that slows gymnasts down.

When gymnasts perform on the bars, the effects of friction can be even more dramatic. Gymnasts grip the bars and turn around them in giant swings to gain momentum. As they turn, their hands rub on the bars, creating friction and

---

ROUND OFF

3 seconds

Amount of time gymnasts must stand on both feet after ending a trampoline routine.

ANGULAR MOMENTUM, GRAVITY, AND "THE GIANT"

"The Giant" is a common gymnastics move that involves many physics principles. The momentum created by the gymnast's body during the first half of the swing and the "tap" must counteract friction between the gymnast's hands and the bar, and the force of gravity as the body swings back to the top of the circle.

1 Momentum is created by the fall of the gymnast's body as it descends during the first half of the swing. Gravity pulls the body towards the ground, creating some of the speed needed to complete this move.

3 Fighting the force of gravity on the final section of "the Giant", the gymnast will bend his or her body at both the shoulders and the hips. By shortening the circumference of the circle created by the body around the bar, the gymnast will increase his or her angular velocity and, if successful, retain enough momentum to overcome gravity.

2 At the bottom of the swing, the gymnast will perform what is known as the "tap" – by slightly arching the back and using muscle strength to powerfully and quickly swing the legs forward, the gymnast creates additional momentum.

Modified Gymnastics

Most gymnasts depend on their vision when they train and compete. Blind gymnasts do not have that ability. They can still perform in the sport. They just need some modifications that allow them to use senses other than vision.

According to the United States Association of Blind Athletes, blind gymnasts need modifications for balance beam, floor exercises and vault. When learning to perform on the beam, a sighted coach can tell them if they are in danger of going off the end. As they gain experience, however, blind gymnasts gain a sense of the length of the beam and only need verbal cues if they make a mistake.

During floor exercises, blind gymnasts run the risk of going off the mat without realizing it. They use sound to indicate the point where they should turn around. During training a coach might call out to indicate the turn around point. In competition, a tape recorder playing music can do the job.

To learn to vault, blind gymnasts work on dismounts first. That gives them time to understand the height of the vault. When they move on to mounting, they count their steps as they run. Then the coach slaps the top of the vault. Blind gymnasts use their sense of hearing to find the vault in space and place their hands on it properly.

resistance. With practice, elite gymnasts learn how to grip the bars tightly enough to stay on the bars and in control while in motion. At the same time, they keep their hands loose enough to slide easily on the bars.

Elite gymnasts cannot risk having their hands stick or slip. A wrong move could easily break up the routine and throw off their rhythm, causing them to slow down and lose momentum. In order to earn a high score in competition, gymnasts need to take advantage of the speed and momentum they are creating. "On bars, if you have a break early, getting back into the rhythm of your routine is usually difficult. Since so much of a bar routine relies on the speed and momentum generated from giant swings, when you have to

ROUND OFF

10 feet

Height that elite gymnasts can find themselves in the air when dismounting the bars with an aerial move.

start all over after a break, it's difficult to get that speed and momentum back," Olympic gymnast Kerri Strug says. "You also have to have a certain feel, or flow, during a bar routine, or you can suffer the consequences."[22]

Performing in the Air

Difficult gymnastics moves can start on the floor or on apparatus like the vault, bars, or beam. Gymnasts may push off from a standing position or gain momentum from turns on the bar, then let go to become airborne. As gymnasts launch into the air in a spin off the uneven bars, they use angular momentum. Once gymnasts are in the air, angular momentum remains constant. It cannot be increased or decreased because there is not anything solid in the air to push off from.

Still, gymnasts need a way to gain speed so they can spin and flip while airborne. They need to increase their spinning speed, or angular velocity, by pulling their limbs in and creating a more compact shape, which will be less resistant to acceleration. The speed of spinning can be calculated by dividing the measurement of a circle by the time it takes to complete a full revolution. There are 360 degrees in a circle. If gymnasts complete one revolution (360 degrees) in four seconds, they are spinning at a rate of 90 degrees per second.

Working Blind

Creating angular velocity is not the only challenge gymnasts encounter when performing airborne tricks. Naturally gymnasts must take their eyes off the apparatus they are using to perform flips and rotations. To complete the move, they must relocate the apparatus while in motion and land flawlessly to maintain their rhythm and continue their routine. For example, when gymnasts perform aerials such as hands-free front and backflips on the beam, they also have to figure out how to land back on the beam before they actually see it.

During flips and rotations, gymnasts must take their eyes off the apparatus and relocate it—while still in motion—in order to complete the move.

Olympic gymnast Kurt Thomas explains, "If you depend on your eyes to tell you where you are, all you see is a blur of walls, lights, and faces. Some gymnasts count to themselves, 'One … two … three,' in order to anticipate their landing. But over the years I seem to have acquired an air sense of where I am at all times during a trick."[23]

Proprioception, or a sense of their body in space, helps elite gymnasts stay oriented while adjusting their form and body positioning in the air. According to Olympic gymnast Nadia Comaneci, aerials on the beam are a particularly difficult skill to master. "I always knew when I was crooked going into an aerial on the beam," she says. "Just like all elite gymnasts, I'd make tiny corrections while in the air. Those split-second judgments made the difference between falling off the beam and hurting myself or completing a successful skill that allowed me to win competitions."[24]

Making Gymnastics Equipment Safer

Within the past ten years the rules for the design and use of gymnastics apparatus have changed and become safer for athletes. For example gymnasts used to perform vaults using a horse. The trick was dangerous even in practice. "The horse used to be long and skinny, with only a limited space to put your hands. When you are doing a flip-flop onto it, you basically have to go to the right spot every single time, and that was a little scary," Olympic gymnast Carly Patterson told Time magazine in 2008. "A lot of times, I would see people's hands slipping off, or missing the horse completely."

In 2001 the horse was replaced with the wider and safer vault used today. Rules have also changed to require a mat in front of the vault. The mat surrounds the springboard where gymnasts launch. It can provide protection in case gymnasts slip or fall.

Some people in the gymnastics community would like to see more steps taken to prepare athletes for gymnastics and make the sport safer. "There are a lot of things that have been done to make gymnastics safer, but you can

In 2001, the long, skinny vaulting horse was replaced with a wider and safer vaulting table (pictured).

always do more," says Olympic gymnast Shannon Miller.

Quoted in Alice Park, "Making Gymnastics Safer for Kids," *Time*, April 8, 2008, www.time.com/time/health/article/0,8599,1728902,00.html.

Tiny corrections and split-second judgments are determining factors in competitions at the highest levels. Winning requires performing with absolute precision. Throughout a routine or even one trick, elite gymnasts have to get each move right from beginning to end. They work to perfect timing, body positioning, speed, and momentum. They also have to adjust each element based on how a move progresses in the moment. "There's such a major difference between a [score of] 9.8 and a 9.9, and it all has to do with how technically clean you are," Retton says. "Every little mistake—a wobble on the beam, a hop on the landing, a slipped hand on the bars—can cost you a tenth of a point, and in our sport, that's the difference between first and second [place]."[25]

Landing Forces

The final element of a gymnastics routine is the dismount, or landing. Gymnasts must "stick" their landing to earn a good score in competition. That means landing on their feet and stopping motion immediately. Even when dismounting from apparatus like the vault, bars, or beam, they cannot hop around or take a step to stabilize their bodies.

Newton's first law of motion—an object in motion tends to stay in motion—is one reason landing from an airborne trick is so difficult. Kinetic energy is difficult to stop. Momentum will work to keep gymnasts moving while they try to end their routine.

Elite gymnasts struggle with landings just like less-experienced gymnasts. In fact, top gymnasts have to work even harder to control landing forces because they use more angular velocity, reach greater heights, and gain more momentum to perform their moves. Those factors create more powerful landing forces, which include contact force and impact force.

Contact force is the result of two objects coming in contact. Impact force is determined by the mass of a gymnast's body, the speed at which his or her body is falling, and how gravity is working to accelerate that speed. When gymnasts stick a good landing, they control kinetic energy. They also control and absorb landing forces. Landing hard at the end of a trick produces forces that can knock gymnasts off balance and cause injury.

Sticking It

While true perfection is rarely possible during a gymnastics performance, gymnasts at every level strive to land with control and precision. When gymnasts prepare to dismount from an apparatus, they use angular momentum just like

Repeatedly practicing landings prepares gymnasts to do whatever they can to stick their landing.

Gymnast Turned Diver

Many gymnasts take what they learn in gymnastics and apply it to other sports when they want to try something new. Maribeth Smith was a gymnast for twelve years, starting when she was just two years old. Then she broke her back and was not able to continue doing gymnastics.

Once Smith healed from her injury, she decided to try diving instead. When she was a student at Marshall University, in Huntington, West Virginia, she joined the school's swimming and diving team. While taking up a new sport presented some challenges, Smith found the basics were easy to master. As a gymnast, she already had a well-developed sense of body awareness. She also had plenty of experience performing flips.

"I didn't want to stop competing," Smith says. "Diving was the closest thing to gymnastics that I could do, with less impact."

Maribeth Smith, phone interview with the author, October 2009.

Gymnasts can apply the skills they've learned to other sports, such as diving.

they did at the beginning of their routine. This time, however, they need to decrease their angular velocity to gain control over their landing. They stretch their bodies open to increase the distance between their center of gravity and the axis of movement. This slows them down, so they can spend more time in the air before hitting the mat on the ground.

Gymnasts take that time to prepare for their landing. In a split second, gymnasts adjust their body so they will land with their center of gravity best positioned for balance. They are less likely to be thrown off balance if landing forces are distributed evenly throughout their body. Other factors can come into play, however. Even landing with one foot on a seam on the mat can alter body positioning enough to create an uneven distribution of landing forces.

When gymnasts finally do hit the mat, they bend at the knees, ankles, and hips. In this stable position, they can absorb the impact of the landing forces before straightening up to a standing position. Strong muscles and flexibility help gymnasts stick a good landing and avoid injury from the impact.

Even in the worst conditions, elite gymnasts are prepared to do whatever they can to stick their landing. They practice landings over and over, and they know just what to do when a perfect landing is impossible. When Strug performed her gold-medal vault in the 1996 Olympics, she had a severe ankle injury. She kept going, made decisions based on the circumstances, and managed to stick her landing on one foot. "I slammed into the floor a little short [of the proper position], but clean, and immediately, I heard another big rip in my ankle. I thought for sure my leg had snapped in two," she says. "Instinctively, maybe because I had done it thousands of times since the first time [my sister] Lisa showed me when I was three years old, I hopped into the finishing pose. I did it standing on just my right foot, like a flamingo. But I threw my shoulders back, stuck out my chin, stretched out my arms, and saluted the judges."[26]

CHAPTER 5

Injuries and Treatments

According to a 2008 study of gymnastics injuries conducted by researchers at Nationwide Children's Hospital in Columbus, Ohio, gymnasts are just as likely to be injured as athletes who play basketball, ice hockey, and soccer.

Most gymnasts know they will sustain injuries. "If you're doing it right, everything from your little toe to your little finger is constantly in motion," Olympic gymnast Shannon Miller says. "Everything is flipping, moving or turning. It works the entire body in a way no other sport does, and the more body parts that are moving, the more you are open to injuries."[27] Most gymnasts hope their injuries will be minor rather than severe, but they have to be aware of how injuries are caused in order to try to prevent them.

Minor Injuries

When beginner gymnasts are hurt, their injuries are usually minor and common to the sport. For example, when gymnasts are in motion, they can easily catch a finger on an apparatus. Due to momentum and Newton's first law of motion (an object in motion tends to stay in motion), the gymnast's body will keep moving forward while the finger is caught. That can result in a dislocated bone, which means the bone is pushed out of position at the joint. It could also result in a broken finger.

A dislocated finger looks deformed, but it can often be pulled back into place. If the finger is broken, the gymnast will feel even more pain and can expect swelling, too. A lot of swelling may cause numbness, as nerves in the hand are compressed. A broken finger can be diagnosed by an X-ray at the hospital and may need a splint to hold it still while it heals.

The effects of friction also cause minor injuries to beginners as well as more experienced gymnasts. When they train and perform, gymnasts' hands and feet rub on apparatus like the bars and the beam. Their feet drag slightly on the mats as they land and absorb the impact. "On bars you're always ripping your hands [creating blisters that rip open] and building

The friction from an athlete's hands rubbing on the bars and beam can cause minor injuries.

up callus from all the twisting and the friction," Olympic gymnast Mary Lou Retton says. "I had to put Vaseline and vitamin E on them and wear tube socks with holes cut out at night."[28]

Getting Ripped

The friction that results when gymnasts come in contact with apparatus and mats causes heat and irritates the skin. That can cause blisters that may eventually rip open. After repeating movements over and over, gymnasts also develop a callus, or thick layer of protective skin, on areas of their hands and feet. Calluses can only provide limited protection. As gymnasts continue their intense training, friction causes calluses to tear off, too.

The best treatment for a ripped blister or callus starts before the rip happens. To prevent rips, gymnasts use lotion on their hands and feet to keep the skin moist. They also try to stop too much callus from building up. They soak their hands in water and rub off the callused area with a pumice stone.

When a callus or blister does rip, gymnasts have to make sure all of the loose skin is removed so the skin does not harden and press painfully into the open wound. They either pull the skin off or cut it with sterile scissors. Then they wash the area and use antibacterial ointment to prevent an infection. Finally they tape it up with a sterile bandage so they can get back to practice.

Bruising on Impact

Working with hard surfaces and wooden equipment, gymnasts also have to deal with bruising. When they make a mistake, they might be knocked into an apparatus or onto the floor. How much force they land with depends on several different factors. Speed can affect the force of impact. A gymnast running toward the vault at a fast rate of speed will crash with more impact than a gymnast running slower.

ROUND OFF

425,900

Number of children ages six to seventeen who were treated in United States hospital emergency rooms for gymnastics-related injuries between 1990 and 2005.

Increased velocity results in more kinetic energy and forward momentum.

Falling from a height also changes conditions that alter the force of impact, which is determined by calculating the mass of the gymnast's body, velocity, and gravitational acceleration. If a gymnast falls from the bars, for example, the force of gravity will increase kinetic energy. That accelerates the speed of the fall and increases the impact. In addition, gymnasts will fall faster if they are spinning in a tuck rather than stretched out parallel to the ground. In a tuck, they have less surface area to be slowed by the air's resistance. In other words, they have lower inertia and a higher rate of angular velocity in a tuck.

Working Through the Pain

Minor injuries like dislocated fingers, rips, and bruises are not debilitating, and they do not usually have long-lasting effects. They still hurt, however. Beginners may feel discouraged or frustrated by minor injuries.

Gymnasts who want to compete at the elite level realize dealing with pain is a part of the sport. They force themselves to keep training and performing despite their discomfort, sometimes even when the injury is more serious.

When a blister or callus rips, a gymnast must remove the loose skin so it does not harden and press painfully into the open wound.

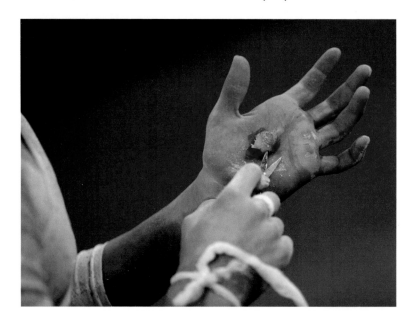

THE IMPACT OF LANDING

In gymnastics, falls are not the only mishaps that can lead to serious injury. An improper landing from a dismount can result in broken bones, sprained ankles, or damaged knee tendons and ligaments. A tear of the anterior cruciate ligament (ACL), for instance, can be both painful and career-ending.

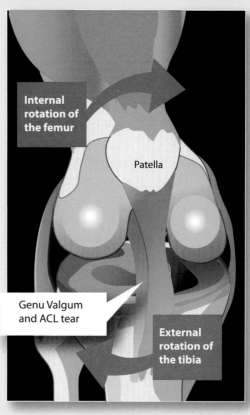

Internal rotation of the femur

Patella

Genu Valgum and ACL tear

External rotation of the tibia

Gymnast off balance, falling forward

Internal rotation of the femur

External rotation of the tibia

When gymnast Alyssa Beckerman, a former member of the U.S. national team, broke her wrist, she kept training and competing on it for forty hours each week for a year. "Everyone is in pain," Olympic medalist Courtney Kupets told *International Gymnast* magazine in an interview in 2009. "We're gymnasts, and we're going to have injuries, so it's just a matter of how headstrong you are to get through them."[29]

Throughout her career in gymnastics, Kupets has endured major injuries, including torn Achilles tendons and a hip fracture. Although one injury kept her out of gymnastics for

Many gymnasts who compete at the elite level force themselves to keep training despite sometimes serious injuries like a broken wrist.

part of the 2008 season, she did not want to quit. "I've done gymnastics my entire life, and I wasn't going to go out on an injury," she says. "I wanted to go out doing big gymnastics, having fun and doing all for events, of course. I did the same thing before the 2004 Olympics. I tore my Achilles' tendon and was back in six months."[30]

Japanese gymnast Shun Fujimoto is famous for helping his team earn a gold medal at the 1976 Olympics by competing with a broken kneecap. After breaking his kneecap during floor exercises, he went on to compete on the pommel horse and rings without mentioning his injury to his coach. The injury was extremely painful and ended his career as a gymnast. He later said that if he had it to do over again, he would not continue competing while injured.

Serious Injuries

At every level gymnasts practice and compete knowing their sport can cause injuries. Most major injuries can be avoided, however, when gymnasts take the proper preventative measures. Warming up and stretching prepares muscles to handle the physical activity to come. Focusing carefully on technique is also essential. When gymnasts pay attention to messages from their proprioceptors, they are less likely to make mistakes.

As gymnasts advance in the sport, however, they perform increasingly dangerous skills. More difficult moves require more speed, height, and momentum, putting them at greater physical risk. While they strive for perfection, injuries are always possible, even—and perhaps especially—for the best athletes.

Physical Therapists

Physical therapists treat people who have problems with mobility. They help patients stretch and move to overcome their conditions over a recommended period of time, so patients will experience less pain and, hopefully, regain the ability to move normally. The treatments physical therapists provide may also include teaching patients how to use mobility equipment such as walkers and crutches.

Physical therapists are highly educated professionals who have a bachelor's degree and a master's or doctoral degree in physical therapy. Their education includes science courses, such as biology, chemistry, and physics, and they learn about biomechanics, neuroanatomy, and human development. They also complete training in how to examine and treat patients.

Before physical therapists can treat patients, they must pass national and state exams in order to obtain a license to practice in their state. Continuing education is also part of the job. Some states require continuing education to maintain a license. In addition, physical therapists can best treat their patients when they have up-to-date information about research and new developments in their field. The American Physical Therapy Association, a national professional organization, offers courses helpful to physical therapists who treat injured gymnasts, such as sports physical therapy, hand rehabilitation, and orthopedics, the science of the skeletal system.

Continuing education is an important part of treating athletes in sports physical therapy.

In order to reach and compete at the highest level, elite gymnasts have been known to overwork their bodies. Many have sustained stress fractures as a result of overtraining to be the best. A stress fracture is a break in the bone that results from repetitive motion and low force of impact. Olympic gymnast Kelly Garrison sustained twenty-two stress fractures in her back throughout her career.

Elite gymnasts also typically undergo several surgeries throughout their career to repair a variety of major injuries, such as torn muscles, inflamed tendons, and badly broken bones. When Olympic gold medalist Paul Hamm fractured his hand falling off the parallel bars, for example, he needed surgery to insert a metal plate and nine screws to secure the bone. The plate and screws held the bone in place so that it could heal properly.

Some gymnasts have paid an even higher price in their quest for success in the sport. In 2006 top Welsh gymnast Chris Fordham died after falling from a trampoline during practice. He miscalculated his dismount and hit the floor, fracturing his skull on impact.

Stopping to Heal

Ambitious gymnasts may be tempted to keep training and competing even while injured. In the end, however, that can worsen the original injury or lead to a secondary injury, which means the first injury causes another. An injured hip, for example, could interfere with the biomechanics of how a gymnast moves. As a result, the gymnast could eventually develop a back injury.

Olympic gymnast Kerri Strug dealt with a major injury when she was training to compete in Europe before the 1996 Olympics. While doing some pull-ups, she pulled a stomach muscle. She tried to ignore the pain and continue working out, even though the pain got worse each day. She even ignored the advice of a doctor who recommended that she take at least a week off to heal. During the competition in Europe, she injured herself again, and this time it was a more serious injury.

"I felt a big rip on my left side. I knew immediately that I had torn the muscle. It was like something was slicing my stomach in half, unzipping it from the bottom to the top,"[31] she says.

ROUND OFF

Most elite gymnasts competing for the U.S. national team from 1982 to 2004 continued training on injuries or without a doctor's consent, according to a study by the *Orange County Register* newspaper.

Putting Off Puberty

Training too much and eating too little can decrease the estrogen levels in a female gymnast's blood. That can lead to delayed menstruation. And that can be a problem, because girls have their final growth spurt when they begin menstruating. If menstruation does not begin when it should—because a gymnast is overworked or too thin—the gymnast risks decreasing or losing out on that growth spurt altogether. When gymnasts start puberty late due to poor health, their bodies still grow and develop, but they may wind up shorter than normal in stature.

Gymnasts with low estrogen also lose bone density and that can lead to stress fractures and osteopenia, a condition where a gymnast has abnormally low bone density for her age. Some young female gymnasts have the bone density of a woman in her seventies or eighties. When they stop training and their estrogen level increases, they can regain some bone density. Bone loss can also be treated with extra daily doses of calcium and vitamin D, as well as prescription medications.

A major injury like Strug's will sideline even the most determined athlete. Strug was horrified when doctors told her she would have to wait six months before competing again after her injury. Other top gymnasts have found themselves in similar predicaments. When Paul Hamm was training for the 2008 Olympics, he was dealing with the pain from his fractured hand, a shoulder injury, and a schedule of nonstop training. He wound up withdrawing from the team.

Gymnast Shayla Worley was also sidelined by injury. She was working toward a spot on the U.S. Olympic women's gymnastics team in 2008 when she felt a pop in her leg during warm-ups on the balance beam. She had fractured her right fibula, a bone in the leg below the knee, and could not continue competing.

Worley retired from elite gymnastics at that point and planned another path instead. "After a lot of thought and talking to my family and coaches, I decided it would be best for my body and my gymnastics career to prepare for my collegiate season," she says. "I plan to start at the University of Georgia and compete on the Gym Dogs gymnastics team in the fall of 2009."[32]

Making a Comeback

Competing at any level after an injury is not easy. In most cases a serious injury requires gymnasts to rest and take time off from physical activity. That prescription enhances the healing process, but elite gymnasts cannot afford to take time away from the gym. Without regular workouts, they will quickly gain weight and lose muscle tone and flexibility.

Most major injuries can heal, however, with time, rest, and sometimes surgery to repair the damage. Once they heal, physical therapy helps gymnasts regain muscle tone, flexibility, and technical skills.

Physical therapy for gymnasts typically involves strength training exercises. Gymnasts may do simple exercises like lunges and push-ups to build muscle. They might also add weights to create more resistance and build more muscle.

Sometimes electrical stimulation is used on damaged tissue. When electrical stimulation is used, electrodes are placed on the gymnast's body. An electrical current stimulates muscle to contract, which will help it to grow. The stimulation also improves blood flow to the area.

It takes time and patience for a gymnast to make a full recovery. Returning to gymnastics can feel like starting over as a beginner, even for an athlete who formerly competed at the highest level. After her stomach injury, Strug followed a physical therapy program that included deep massages and electrical stimulation. Three months passed before she could return to the gym. She also found a new coach who understood the kind of training she needed to make a full comeback. "The process was so slow, but I knew I was doing things the right way. I relearned all the compulsory routines. I added some new elements. Until the doctors cleared me, all I could do was handstands and cartwheels," she says. "Things worked out well when I began going full speed in the gym. Before I knew it, I felt stronger than I had in more than two years."[33]

CHAPTER 6

The Psychology of Gymnastics

While gymnasts are capable of performing amazing feats, they are still regular people with normal fears, anxieties, hopes, and dreams. When they prepare to compete, they have to get excited enough to get their adrenaline pumping. They also have to manage their energy level. If they get too keyed up, gymnasts may become nervous. That could cause them to lose control of their moves or freeze up before performing.

Realizing the potential for failure, gymnasts sometimes naturally feel afraid. They worry about making mistakes and being injured. They fear losing the respect of their teammates and coaches. They are troubled by the possibility they will disappoint their families if they do not perform well. At the elite level, parents often spend thousands of dollars to get their children the right gymnastics training. The pressure on an elite gymnast is enormous. "I have always been bothered by those parents who pick up and move everyone and everything to another city, just for the sake of their child's dream. To me, that's too much," Olympic gymnast Kerri Strug says. "Not only are you telling your kid that his or her whole life should be whatever the sport is, but you're telling him or her that all of your lives are devoted to that sport too. Talk about pressure."[34]

Gymnasts must manage their energy levels to prevent nerves that could cause them to lose control during performances.

Despite the pressures, gymnasts perform anyway. They run toward the vault at top speed, aware of the dangers as momentum carries them forward. They dismount from the bars knowing a fall from that height would have a painful force of impact. They leap in the air from the balance beam, even though a bad landing could send them to the hospital with severe injuries.

In the best circumstances, gymnasts are able to overcome their worries by combining their own desires to succeed with

The Brain on Fear

When gymnasts are afraid to try a difficult trick or fear losing to another competitor, their emotions can work in their favor. Fear causes the brain to release dopamine, norepinephrine, and endorphins. These chemicals are a combination of hormones and neurotransmitters, which help brain cells communicate.

Dopamine is a neurotransmitter that creates good feelings. Norepinephrine is a hormone and neurotransmitter that fills gymnasts with energy. Endorphins are hormones and neurotransmitters that relieve pain, so gymnasts are not limited by physical discomfort. Put them all together, and these brain chemicals push gymnasts to give an even better performance.

support from family members, coaches, and teammates. They face their fears head on and perform to the best of their abilities in spite of them. "I don't give up, ever. I don't run away from a challenge because I am afraid," Olympic gymnast Nadia Comaneci says. "Instead, I run toward it because the only way to escape fear is to trample it beneath your feet."[35]

Falling in Love with Gymnastics

Many top gymnasts fell in love with gymnastics when they were very young. Even injury and moments of failure and struggle do not discourage them from sticking with it.

Some gymnasts grow up with the sport and can barely remember life without it. Olympic gymnast Dominique Moceanu was pushed into the sport. Even before she was born, Moceanu's father was determined that his daughter would be an athlete. He began her training when she was a toddler. He tested her strength by having her hang onto a clothesline as long as she could.

Comaneci joined her first gymnastics team while in kindergarten. "My mother took me to the large gymnasium where the team practiced because she wanted to find out outlet for my excessive energy.... I still loved soccer, but gymnastics slowly began to eclipse all other sports in my life," Comaneci says. "It's a history I find difficult to recall because I was only six years old when it all began for me."[36]

Olympic gymnast Kurt Thomas, on the other hand, started gymnastics when he was a teenager. At fourteen, he was 4 feet, 9 inches tall (1.4m) and 77 pounds (35kg). He was small for his age and wanted to find a sport that matched his body type. After watching a college gymnastics team practice, he was inspired to start a gymnastics team at his high school. It took some time and practice, but he began to win at gymnastics competitions. By his senior year, he was so excited about the sport, he stayed behind to be near his gym when his family moved away. He recalls, "A friend [and I] rented a house and lived in it by ourselves for six months, doing all the shopping, cooking, and cleaning—and getting jobs on the side to pay for it all."[37]

When gymnasts succeed at the sport, they sometimes start to dream big. They might hope to make it all the way to the Olympics. Some gymnasts get hooked on winning medals and trophies and on receiving positive attention for their talents. If parents and coaches encourage them, they have good reason to keep working toward their goal. When gymnasts feel good about what they are doing, they may not care why they began in the sport in the first place. "I really enjoy competing, and I'm having fun," Moceanu told the *New York Times* when she was thirteen. "That's what it's all about. If that's what people remember me for, then that's great."[38]

Force of Will

Gymnasts who feel strongly about advancing in their sport often want intensive training with the best coaches. That usually means leaving home to live with another family or even their coach. These gymnasts make major decisions about their own lives while still teenagers or even younger. They show unusual maturity by knowing what they want most in life. They are able to focus and work toward a long-term goal.

Even before they start serious training, however, gymnasts need a naturally strong will. They have to fight against social norms and family pressure. Strug was twelve when she realized she felt unprepared in competition. She dreamed of one day making it to the Olympics, so she told her parents she wanted to leave their home in Tucson, Arizona, to train with coach Bela Karolyi in Houston, Texas. "I made a list, of course. I outlined all the positives and negatives. All I had was positives. I told them that I wanted to be one of the best, so I should train with the best," she says. "On and on I went, nonstop every day."[39]

Strug's parents worried she would not be able to handle living far away from them and working so hard at gymnastics. Eventually, however, Strug wore them down. They said yes, and she was allowed to go soon after turning thirteen. "I was petrified and thrilled at the same time,"[40] she says.

Young gymnasts may have their own lingering doubts. They know advancing in the sport will require making sacrifices. Many gymnasts decide to accept that and fight for their long-term goals. Olympic gymnast Mary Lou Retton was fourteen when she decided to leave home, also to train with Karolyi. Her parents let her make the decision, and she felt she understood the consequences. "Nobody likes to leave home for a long period of time, especially when you're a teenager. Everything you've ever known is there—your family, your friends, your school, all the places you hang around," she says. "But by the end of 1982, I knew in my heart I had to leave there if I wanted to become the best gymnast I could.... I knew that if I didn't go, I'd never really know whether I could have made it to the Olympics. For the rest of my life I would have thought, well, I could have made it if.... There always would have been that *if.*"[41]

Honing the Competitive Edge

Some gymnasts are driven by the idea of mastering their craft. Others strive to avoid letting down their parents, coaches, and teammates. Many are inspired by the challenges created by strong competition.

Often gymnasts cannot push themselves to greater success when they train in isolation. "I needed someone pushing and pushing me, and I needed some other girls around me who were shooting for the same thing I was," Retton says. "I didn't know Bela [Karolyi] at all, but I'd seen his girls and I was impressed. They were so ready and confident, and Bela was always beside them, getting them hyped up … he had them so mentally prepared that they had no doubts."[42]

Gymnasts train with other athletes because they can push each other to greater success.

Many top training programs for gymnasts are based on creating a competitive environment. Karolyi is famous for using this approach to get into the minds of his gymnasts. "The only thing that consistently works with kids is to stand behind them, motivate them, make them excited. You show the challenge, make them feel confident, and that makes them to be going further and further all the time,"[43] Karolyi says.

Not all coaches are known for creating a psychologically healthy environment for their gymnasts, however. In fact, Karolyi himself came under criticism from gymnasts, parents, the media, and other trainers in the 1990s. Author Joan Ryan writes,

> Karolyi constructed a training environment that kept his star athlete questioning her worth. In selecting five other gymnasts to train with her, he carefully chose each to play a specific role. Perhaps the most torturous position was that of the secondary star: like the understudy in a play, the girl was just talented enough to present a threat to the star's status. He would play all six girls like chess pieces, every move designed to toughen and sharpen the queen. He would pit them against each other. Karolyi would shun one girl in order to teach another a lesson. He'd make one gymnast do extra work for a teammate's mistakes. Karolyi would also have a group of younger gymnasts, his next generation of stars, training at the gym to keep the pressure on his top six.[44]

Under Pressure

Once gymnasts leave home to train seriously, the pressure to succeed increases dramatically. Most children and teenagers spend years trying different activities to see what they like. For serious gymnasts, that is not an option. Taking time away from gymnastics for any reason could easily set them back so far they cannot recover.

When gymnasts are working toward a particular competition, they cannot afford to lose training time. Even when a competition is not approaching immediately, the pressure is particularly intense for female gymnasts throughout their gymnastics career. Female gymnasts' bodies change dramatically with the onset of puberty. Once they develop hips and breasts, their bodies are not as light and streamlined. They will have more weight to bring into the air when they leap and flip. They might also have to deal with more height. These gymnasts know they have to do their best work before puberty hits.

Women also have a higher percentage of body fat than men after puberty. "Men can get by with ten to fifteen percent body fat and be really fit. Some men are able to go to five percent and in some cases a little less than that and still maintain excellent health," explains Matthew Goodemote, a physical therapist. "Woman under ten percent [body fat] often stop having their periods or have them inconsistently. Under five percent is getting serious if not dangerous."[45]

As puberty approaches, female gymnasts experience psychological changes as well. Young girls tend to lose confidence when their bodies change. That puts them at risk when unethical coaches use their feelings against them. "Studies show that a young girl's self-esteem plummets much more dramatically than that of a boy at a similar stage in life," writes Ryan. "Self-conscious about her looks and sensitive about her body, in particular her weight, she is a mass of insecurities looking for an identity. She is the perfect clay with which coaches can create the ideal gymnast."[46]

ROUND OFF

60%

Percentage of gymnasts who were either too afraid to tell their coaches when they were injured or they were verbally abused when they did, according to a 2004 *Orange County Register* survey.

Scare Tactics

An elite gymnast's intense training generally involves a strict schedule that includes several hours in the gym each day. Some coaches use that busy schedule to gain control of their gymnasts' minds. They might isolate their gymnasts from family and friends. Some tell their gymnasts that they are too fat and demand that they lose weight, even when they are actually underweight for their height. There are also coaches who use a variety of bullying tactics to control athletes, such as verbal abuse, swearing, and physical violence.

Many elite gymnasts who trained in the 1980s and 1990s report that popular coaching methods at the time exploited their insecurities. Michelle Hilse, a former member of the U.S. Gymnastics Team , told the *Orange County Register* newspaper that her coach hit her when she approached him after breaking her hand during practice. Hilse recalls, "He yelled, 'Get out of my face.' Then he slapped my head and yelled, 'Stop your crying.' "[47]

Some coaches use verbal abuse and other bullying tactics to control athletes.

Moceanu also reported abuse from her coaches. Years after helping her team win a gold medal at the 1996 Olympics, she told the *Los Angeles Times* that she was forced to weigh herself in front of the team and was belittled about her weight. Moceanu said she was too afraid to speak out at the time.

Damaging Effects

Psychological abuse can be just as damaging to gymnasts as physical abuse. When gymnasts are verbally abused or fear physical abuse, they may feel nervous, afraid, and upset. They may lose their ability to trust their own judgment or stop listening to other people who care about them. Even the most focused athletes may begin to abuse themselves as a result. That can lead to physical as well as psychological problems.

Some gymnasts push their bodies too hard after an injury or starve themselves to try to achieve the ideal body of a gymnast. Strug once worked with a coach who recommended she lose weight. She began to diet even though she only weighed 85 pounds (39kg) at the time. "I figured I was just losing a couple of pounds. But then I started getting tired and weak. I focused on workouts because I knew that's where I had to perform. But I felt sluggish a lot more during the day and would feel completely exhausted at the end of the day," she says. "Gradually, my body started to feel the effects of my poor eating habits.... Tricks that used to be easy were now impossible."[48]

With help from her family and trainers, Strug was able to turn her situation around. Not all gymnasts have the mental strength and support to do the same, however. Gymnast Christy Henrich took it to heart when a judge told her she needed to lose weight to make it to the Olympics. Henrich had already expressed concerns to her coach that she was not thin and lean enough to compete in the sport.

She dropped from 90 to 80 pounds (41kg to 36kg) and praise from her coach encouraged her to lose more. She kept losing weight and strength and soon retired from gymnastics altogether. Heinrich had anorexia nervosa, an eating

EFFECTS OF ANOREXIA ON THE BODY

Many gymnasts feel pressure to strictly control their eating habits in order to maintain a low body weight. But starving the body of essential nutrients, such as with anorexia nervosa, can have devastating effects.

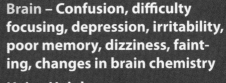

Brain – Confusion, difficulty focusing, depression, irritability, poor memory, dizziness, fainting, changes in brain chemistry

Hair – Hair loss

Heart – Irregular heartbeat (arrhythmia), low blood pressure, slow heart rate, possible heart failure

Blood – Low iron (anemia), loss of essential nutrients

Muscles and Bones – Muscle weakness, swollen joints, low bone density (osteopenia), danger of developing osteoporosis

Kidneys – Kidney stones, possible kidney failure

Digestive System – Constipation, bloating, stomach pain

Hormones – Slowed physical development in adolescents, low estrogen levels, loss of regular menstrual cycles (amenorrhea), fertility problems

Skin – Excessive bruising, dry and yellow skin, growth of fine hair (lanugo) all over the body, a feeling of coldness, brittle nails

Working with Sports Psychologists

When gymnasts get ready to perform, physiological changes take place. Their heart rate and breathing rate increase. They may start to sweat. These physical symptoms can make even an elite gymnast too nervous to perform. That's when a sports psychologist can help.

According to Cory Bank, a sports psychologist and founder of the Abington Center for Therapy and Sports Psychology, in Glenside, Pennsylvania, gymnasts can improve performance by learning to create a better mental experience. One method involves relabeling physical experiences. For example, a gymnast will feel energized rather than fearful when a fast heart rate is labeled a symptom of excitement, not nervousness. Progressive relaxation can also help. In this approach, gymnasts learn to close their eyes, focus on their breathing and heart rate, and progressively tense and relax muscles throughout their body. Visualization is one more method gymnasts use to maximize their potential. They imagine going through a move or routine with positive results every step of the way.

"Using a sports psychologist gives gymnasts an edge," Banks explains. "It's just another way to achieve the best performance."

Cory Bank, phone interview with author, September 2009.

disorder caused by mental and emotional problems that is characterized by an obsession with losing weight. Her condition spiraled out of control until she weighed less than 50 pounds (23kg). She eventually died, in 1994, of multiple organ failure resulting from her dramatic weight loss. In the article "Dying for a Medal" in a 1994 issue of *People* magazine, journalist William Plummer writes,

Indeed, gymnastics seems designed for [anorexia]. According to Dr. Gail Vaughn, a licensed Missouri counselor who treated Henrich during the last year of her life, anorexia preys mainly on young women who balk at becoming adults and starve themselves to stay thin and girlish. This is a virtual description of what today's female gymnast—whose average size declined from 5'3", 105 lbs. in 1976 to 4'9", 88 lbs. in 1992—must do to stay competitive at the highest levels.[49]

Gymnasts Can Gain Control

Most elite gymnasts find ways to manage the mental pressures of intense training. Personality also plays a role in how they react to their coaches and the constant failure that is part of striving to be a better gymnast. "The great ones have kind of a resiliency where they keep bouncing back," says Jay Granat, a sports psychotherapist. "They have the capacity to learn from their mistakes without getting self-critical."[50]

Gymnasts who do not crack under the mental pressure or get upset by negative comments often have established a connection with their coach.

Some gymnasts are able to make a connection with their coaches, so they do not get upset at negative comments. Retton, for example, found she liked Karolyi and his methods, even when he made fun of her weight and yelled at her about her routines. Sometimes she laughed it off. Other times she felt his approach inspired her to push herself to work harder and improve skills. "I realized pretty quickly that our personalities had a lot in common. We're both pretty open and it's not hard to tell how we're feeling just by looking at us," she says. "There were times when I'd come into the gym and see it right in his eyes. 'Oh, gosh,' I'd tell myself. 'Don't mess with him tonight.'"[51]

Other gymnasts use their own mental tricks to keep control of their training schedules, their bodies, and their lives. Comaneci always kept a reserve of energy for herself while training. She would tell Karolyi what she was capable of, knowing she could actually do more. When Karolyi asked for more than Comaneci suggested, he did not realize he was playing into her strategy. "Let's say that I knew that I could do fifteen laps of the stadium. I'd tell Bela I could do ten and give myself some reserve, some padding. Even if he'd say that I should do twelve, that meant I was capable of doing three more," she says. "I worked out in pain, but I knew the difference between pain that was tolerable and pain that didn't help me and lessened my abilities. I followed my instincts, as I always have, and they led me to safety.... Bela pushed me hard, but the reason he could never break me is because he never truly knew my limits."[52]

Gymnasts who know how to push themselves and know their own limits can achieve great things in the sport. Olympic gymnast Bart Conner has reflected on the mental tactics that helped him make the 1984 Olympic team after tearing his bicep. He recalls,

An odd sensation came over me, and I thought, "I am going to make that Olympic team in 1984. I am going to march into that stadium." I visualized myself entering the stadium, waving to the crowd, and I could hear the sports announcer saying, "Hey, folks, here comes the American men's team. Seven months ago I never would have believed this, but guess what? Bart Conner is on that team." I planned that out in my mind. There I was with an ice bag on my arm, trying to get to the airport in Tokyo to return to the United States for surgery, and I already visualized how I wanted that scene to play out.[53]

Positive Effects of Gymnastics

Not all gymnastics coaches believe abusive tactics and total control are the best means to create champions, of course. Most understand gymnasts need support from friends and family as well as freedom to determine the direction of their own lives.

Gymnastics coach Liang Chow, for example, did not allow Olympic gymnast Shawn Johnson to train too hard. Her training schedule allowed time for her to attend public school and have a social life. Chow's approach also helped Johnson escape major injuries because she did not train too intensely. "With a loving environment, everyone can do more,"[54] he told *USA Today*.

When coaches are mindful of their gymnasts' mental health, the psychological effects of the sport are positive. Learning new tricks teaches gymnasts perseverance and develops concentration skills. Gymnasts also build self-control and discipline by making sacrifices and keeping their focus. When they eventually master new skills, they gain self-esteem. As gymnasts get better and better, they have more confidence building experiences in the gym. That helps them go even further in the sport.

Part of Comaneci's gymnastics training included work with a team of psychologists. They taught the gymnast to practice routines in her head, to manage frustration levels, and to concentrate under difficult conditions. "There's nothing to do about nerves except to stay focused and know that the feeling will go away once it is replaced by concentration," Comaneci says. "If a gymnast can't replace fear with

ROUND OFF

USA Gymnastics partnered with St. Vincent Sports Performance Center in 2006 to support gymnasts with doctors, trainers, and other specialists, including two sport psychologists.

concentration during a competition, then she will have more problems than a few knots in her stomach."[55]

Even pressure can have a positive effect, according to Retton. "I can't say I like having pressure on me. I don't think anybody does. But somehow it brings out the best in me. There's always that nervous feeling, that twinge in your stomach, and I don't know if it means I'm anxious or just ready to go. But I think it's something that every competitor has, and I need that,"[56] she says.

For many gymnasts, the sport is not just about competing and winning, though. It is also about making friends, using the body, pushing limits, and becoming a true athlete. Whether competing at the beginner or elite level, any gymnast can gain those kinds of benefits from participating in the sport. "People always ask me why I put up with everything, why I subject myself to so much pain and heartbreak," Strug says. "I can't explain the thrill I have always felt when I'm flying through the air, spinning and turning, performing at my very best. When I hit the mat, plant my feet, raise my chin, and thrown out my hands in the finishing pose, it's the greatest adrenaline rush in the world."[57]

NOTES

Chapter 1: An Ancient Sport

1. Joan Ryan, *Little Girls in Pretty Boxes*, New York: Doubleday, 1995, p. 46.
2. Kerri Strug with John Lopez, *Landing on My Feet: A Diary of Dreams*, Kansas City, MO: Andrews McMeel, 1997, p. 15.
3. Mary Lou Retton and Bela Karolyi with John Powers, *Mary Lou: Creating an Olympic Champion*, New York: McGraw-Hill, 1986, p. 35.
4. Nadia Comaneci, *Letters to a Young Gymnast*, New York: Basic Books, 2004, p. 23.
5. Ryan, *Pretty Girls in Little Boxes*, p. 24.
6. Quoted in Jeré Longman and Juliet Macur, "Records Say Chinese Gymnasts May Be Under Age," *New York Times*, July 27, 2008. Available online at www.nytimes.com/2008/07/27/sports/olympics/27gymnasts.html.
7. Kurt Thomas and Kent Hannon, *Kurt Thomas on Gymnastics*, New York: Simon and Schuster, 1980, p. 20.
8. Selena Roberts, "IOC Turns Blind Eye to Controversy over China's Kiddie Gymnasts," *Sports Illustrated*, August 13, 2008. Available online at http://sportsillustrated.cnn.com/2008/olympics/2008/writers/selena_roberts/08/13/china.gymnasts.
9. Quoted in Dan Baynes, "Olympic Gymnasts Won't Chase Perfect 10 as New Scoring Debuts," Bloomburg, August 6, 2008. Available online at www.bloomberg.com/apps/news?pid=20601081&sid=afyDFiqcZDig&refer=australia.
10. Jordan Ellenberg, "Down with the Perfect 10!" Slate, August 12, 2008. Available online at www.slate.com/id/2197336.

Chapter 2: Training and Conditioning

11. Dustyn Roberts, interview with author, June 2009.
12. Retton and Karolyi, *Mary Lou*, p. 76.
13. Kim Rhatigan-Drexler, interview with author.
14. Comaneci, *Letters to a Young Gymnast*, p. 50.
15. Thomas and Hannon, *Kurt Thomas on Gymnastics*, p. 31.

16. Mark Goodemote, interview with author, Gloversville, NY.

Chapter 3: Somersaults, Headstands, and Other Beginner Moves

17. Rhatigan-Drexler, interview with author.
18. Retton and Karolyi, *Mary Lou*, p. 10.
19. Comaneci, *Letters to a Young Gymnast*, pp. 20, 21, 26.
20. Roberts, interview with author.

Chapter 4: Flying High

21. Retton and Karolyi, *Mary Lou*, p. 11.
22. Strug, *Landing on My Feet*, pp. 118–19.
23. Thomas and Hannon, *Kurt Thomas on Gymnastics*, p. 37.
24. Comaneci, *Letters to a Young Gymnast*, p. 151.
25. Retton and Karolyi, *Mary Lou*, p. 20.
26. Strug, *Landing on My Feet*, p. 169.

Chapter 5: Injuries and Treatments

27. Quoted in Alice Park, "Making Gymnastics Safer for Kids," *Time*, April 8, 2008. Available online at www.time.com/time/health/article/0,8599,1728902,00.html.
28. Retton and Karolyi, *Mary Lou*, p. 13.
29. Quoted in John Crumlish, "Interview: Courtney Kupets," *International Gymnast*, March 11, 2009. Available online at www.intlgymnast.com/index.php?option=com_content&view=article&id=798:interview-courtney-kupets-us&catid=3:interviews&Itemid=168.
30. Quoted in Crumlish, "Interview: Courtney Kupets."
31. Strug, *Landing on My Feet*, p. 108.
32. USA Gymnastics, "Shayla Worley Looks Forward to College Career," USA Gymnastics, July 15, 2009. Available at www.usa-gymnastics.org/pages/post.html?PostID=3579&prog=h.
33. Strug, *Landing on My Feet*, pp. 113–14.

Chapter 6: The Psychology of Gymnastics

34. Strug, *Landing on My Feet*, p. 44.
35. Comaneci, *Letters to a Young Gymnast*, p. 69.
36. Comaneci, *Letters to a Young Gymnast*, p. 17.
37. Thomas and Hannon, *Kurt Thomas on Gymnastics*, p. 66.
38. Quoted in *New York Times*, "Gymnastics; Even at Age 13, a Storybook Career Is Emerging," *New York Times*, August 17, 1995. Available online at www.nytimes.com/1995/08/17/sports/gymnastics-even-at-age-13-a-storybook-career-is-emerging.html.

39. Strug, *Landing on My Feet*, pp. 26, 28.
40. Strug, *Landing on My Feet*, p. 28.
41. Retton and Karolyi, *Mary Lou*, pp. 18, 22.
42. Retton and Karolyi, *Mary Lou*, p. 20.
43. Retton and Karolyi, *Mary Lou*, p. 34.
44. Ryan, *Pretty Girls in Little Boxes*, pp. 211–12.
45. Goodemote, interview with author.
46. Ryan, *Pretty Girls in Little Boxes*, p. 205.
47. Quoted in Scott M. Reid, "Gymnasts in Pain: Out of Balance." *Orange County Register*, December 19, 2004.
48. Strug, *Landing on My Feet*, p. 102.
49. William Plummer, "Dying for a Medal," *People*, August 22, 1994. Available online at www.people.com/people/archive/article/0,,20103704,00.html.
50. Jay Granat, interview with author.
51. Retton and Karolyi, *Mary Lou*, pp. 79, 82.
52. Comaneci, *Letters to a Young Gymnast*, p. 91.
53. Bart Conner, "The Crowd Lifted Us Up," America.gov, April 16, 2008. Available online at www.america.gov/st/sports-english/2008/April/20080416141627maduobbA0.2547571.html.
54. Quoted in Marlen Garcia, "Shawn Johnson's Roots Run from Iowa to Beijing," *USA Today*, August 6, 2008. Available online at www.usatoday.com/sports/olympics/beijing/gymnastics/2008-08-06-johnson_N.htm.
55. Comaneci, *Letters to a Young Gymnast*, p. 99.
56. Retton and Karolyi, *Mary Lou*, p. 99.
57. Strug, *Landing on My Feet*, p. 116.

GLOSSARY

aerodynamics: The study of forces on objects moving through the air.

agile: Movements that are quick, skilled, and controlled.

angular velocity: The rate at which an object spins.

biomechanics: The study of how the body moves and how forces act on the body.

center of gravity: An imaginary point in a object where the total weight of the object is concentrated.

cerebellum: Part of the brain that controls unconscious activity.

compulsory: A routine that is the same for each competitor.

drag: Resistance caused by air flow.

fracture: Break.

friction: The resistance that results when the surface of two objects rub against each other.

gravity: A force of attraction between two objects in the universe.

kinetic energy: A form of energy involved in movement.

mass: The amount of matter contained in an object.

momentum: A measure of how an object moves, depending on its mass and velocity.

proprioception: A sense of one's body in space.

spotter: Someone who assists gymnasts to prevent injury during practice.

velocity: A measure of the rate of change in position over a period of time in a particular direction.

weight: A measurement of gravity's force on an object.

Books

Amanda Bader, *Paul and Morgan Hamm: Olympic Heroes*. New York: Razorbill, 2004. A biography of twin gymnasts Paul and Morgan Hamm.

Nadia Comaneci, *Letters to a Young Gymnast*. New York: Basic Books, 2004. Olympic gymnast Nadia Comaneci talks about her experiences growing up in the sport.

Chris Macnab, *Gymnastics*. Broomall, PA: Mason Crest, 2004. A book about preventing and treating gymnastics injuries.

Mary Lou Retton and Bela Karolyi with John Powers, *Mary Lou: Creating an Olympic Champion*. New York: McGraw-Hill, 1986. Olympic gymnast Mary Lou Retton and her coach, Bela Karolyi, detail the events that led up to her gold medal win.

Dean Sewell, Philip Watkins, Murray Griffin, and Ken Roberts, *Sports and Exercise Science: An Introduction*. London: Edward Arnold, 2005. A book that discusses anatomy, metabolism, physiology, nutrition, psychology, and biomechanics in relation to sports, health, and exercise.

Andrew Solway, *Sports Science*. Portsmouth, NH: Heinemann Library, 2009. A book about science and sports.

Kerri Strug, *Landing on My Feet: A Diary of Dreams*. Kansas City. MO: Andrews McMeel, 1997. Olympic gymnast Kerri Strug explains how she persevered in the sport to eventually win a gold medal.

Internet Sources

Inside Gymnastics, "Johnson One Step Closer to Decision on Gym," *Inside Gymnastics*, August 15, 2009, www.insidegymnastics.com/content/show/newsarticle.aspx?articleid=589&zoneid=1.

KidsHealth, "Learning About Proteins," KidsHealth, www.kidshealth.org/kid/stay_healthy/food/protein.html.

Web Sites

International Federation of Gymnastics (www.fig-gymnastics.com). This is the Website for the International Federation of Gymnastics, an organization that oversees international gymnastics. It includes information about rules, scoring, judging, drug use, and the history of the sport.

USA Gymnastics (www.usa-gymnastics.org). This is the Web site of USA Gymnastics, the organization that sets rules and policies for gymnastics in the United States. It includes gymnastics news, information about finding local gymnastics clubs and results of national competitions.

INDEX

Rings, *10, 12, 44*
Ripping blisters and calluses, 60–61, *62*
Romanian gymnasts, 13
Rome, ancient, 9
Routines, 12–13
Russian gymnasts, 13

S

Safety, 54
Scoring, 14, 19–20
Self-esteem, 76
Serious injuries, 64–68
Size of gymnasts, 17–18, 29–33
Slow-twitch muscle fibers, 27
Smith, Maribeth, 57
Somersaults, *40*, 42
Spinning speed, 52
Splits, *8*, 24
Sports psychologists, 80
Springboards, *35, 36, 48*
"Sticking" a landing, *56*, 56–58
Strength training, 25–27
Stress fractures, 65
Stretches, 24–25, 36–37
Strug, Keri, 58, 66–67, 73, 78

T

Terminology, 7, 9
Thomas, Kurt, 31, 72
Training
    age and size, 29–32, *30*
    body weight distribution, 21–22
    competitive edge, 73–75
    endurance, 27
    estrogen levels, 67
    flexibility, 24–25

intensity, 22–24
levels, 42
muscle memory, 46
muscle strength, 25–27
overtraining, 65
practice, 43–46
pressure, 75–76
psychological issues, 31–32
Trampoline, 17, 49
Transverses axis, 42
Tsukahara, Mitsuo, 15
Tumbling, *40*
Twists, *40*

U

USA Gymnastics, 28, 29

V

V sits, 26–27
Vaults
    "The Punch", *48*, 49
    safety, 54, *54*
    Yurchenko vault, 15, *16*
Visualization, 80, 82–83

W

Warming up, 36–38
Weight distribution, 21–22, *22*
Willpower, 72–73
Working blind, 52–54
Worley, Shayla, 67–68

Y

Yurchenko, Natalia, 15, *16*

PICTURE CREDITS

Cover photo: Image copyright Jiang Dao Hua, 2010. Used under license from Shutterstock.com; © 2010 Photos.com, a division of Getty Images. All rights reserved.

© Action Plus Sports Images/Alamy, 60

AP Images, 18, 53

© Bill Bachmann/Alamy, 65

© Cultura RM/Alamy, 70

© David Woolfall/Alamy, 10

© dmac/Alamy, 42

© Duomo/Corbis, 81

Franck Fife/Getty Images, 62

© Gabe Palmer/Alamy, 74

Gale, Cengage Learning, 16, 40, 48, 50, 63, 79

© imagebroker/Alamy, 32, 35

Image copyright Galina Barskaya, 2010. Used under license from Shutterstock.com, 12, 44, 84

Image copyright Jiang Dao Hua, 2010. Used under license from Shutterstock.com, 22

Image copyright Le Do, 2010. Used under license from Shutterstock.com, 64

Image copyright Supri Suharjoto, 2010. Used under license from Shutterstock.com, 77

Image copyright Val Thoermer, 2010. Used under license from Shutterstock.com, 37

© Jochen Tack/Alamy, 57

© MARKA/Alamy, 26

Mark Rolston/AFP/Getty Images, 39

© martin cushen/Alamy, 54

© Neal Preston/Corbis, 8

© Picture Partners/Alamy, 30

Ryan Pierse/Getty Images, 56

© Stock Connection Distribution/Alamy, 24

© Wally McNamee/Corbis, 14

ABOUT THE AUTHOR

Heather E. Schwartz writes about sports, science, and other interesting topics from her home in upstate New York. She enjoys skiing in her free time, and gymnastics is one of her favorite sports to watch. She lives with her husband, Philip, and son, Nolan.